MAKING & USING

TERRARIUMS & PLANTERS

MAKING & USING

TERRARIUMS & PLANTERS

Allen and Stella Daley

Illustrated by
Daphne Freeman
and
Denis Zealley

BLANDFORD PRESS

POOLE · NEW YORK · SYDNEY

Frontispiece
The Victorian and a tall
Diamond Planter with etched
panels.

First published in the U.K.
1986 by Blandford Press,
Link House, West Street,
Poole, Dorset, BH15 1LL.

Distributed in the United
States by Sterling Publishing
Co., Inc., 2 Park Avenue,
New York, N.Y. 10016.

Distributed in Australia by
Capricorn Link (Australia) Pty
Ltd., PO Box 665, Lane Cove,
NSW 2066

**British Library Cataloguing
in Publication Data**

Daley, Allen
    Making and using
    terrariums and planters.
    1. Terrariums
    2. Container gardening
    l. Title   ll. Daley, Stella
    635.9'824   QH68

ISBN 0 7137 1717 3

Typeset by Graphicraft
Typesetters Ltd. Hong Kong

Printed and bound in Hong
Kong by South China Printing
Co.

Contents

Acknowledgements

The authors wish to thank the following people and organisations for their help and time, and permission to reproduce illustrations as shown, willingly given during the research and preparation of this book.

Australian High Commission, British Museum (Natural History), Crafts Council of Victoria, Hartley Wood & Company Limited, J.E. Lighterness, Pilkington Brothers PLC (Figs. 14, 15), Pilkington Glass Museum, Royal Botanical Gardens, Kew, Swiss Glass Engraving Limited (Figs. 35, 36, 37, 38, 39), Victoria and Albert Museum (Fig. 3), Wilsons Glass, Magic Reproductions Limited

The dried and cut flower arrangements were by Elizabeth Heazell, and the technical illustrations by Reginald E. Daley.

The Victorian (Fig. 42) was designed by Kent Lazarus and originally illustrated in *Stained Glass For Plants*, published by Hidden House Publications, USA.

1 History of the Terrarium

Although they are rapidly gaining in popularity, many people have never heard of a terrarium, and certainly do not know of their significant history as the first effective method of transporting plants long distances. The earliest recorded expedition for plant collecting was in Egyptian times. In 1845 B.C., Queen Hatshepsut sent several ships to collect myrrh trees from Somalia (then known as Punt) and bring them back to Egypt. The expedition was successful and produced around thirty trees, all very carefully packed in wicker baskets, which were then suspended on poles.

Such is man's fascination with strange and exotic plants that many

Fig. 1 An illustration from Dr Ward's book Plants in Glazed Cases.

people have, since that time, tried various methods of transporting them from their countries of origin in order to study and endeavour to grow them. The majority of attempts to ship plants, however, invariably ended in most of them perishing. They would die from the varying temperatures encountered on the long voyage, or from being watered too little or too often. The salt spray was not good for them and, of course, if they were protected from this, light was blocked out. Another hazard was that if for any reason at all the voyage was delayed fresh water rations were soon depleted.

This problem presented itself to a M. De Cliex in 1717, when he was in charge of a quantity of coffee plants being shipped to Martinico. He was so mindful of his duty that he shared his own meagre water ration with the sole surviving plant. He eventually delivered this plant to Martinico where, incredibly, it flourished and became the parent stock from which adjacent islands were supplied.

In 1770, John Ellis designed boxes for carrying plants and seedlings from the East Indies and other foreign shores, and in 1825 a horticulturist in Edinburgh hit upon the idea of using a glass case as a window garden. This gentleman, however, A.A. Maconochie, did not inform the public of his invention, nor did he realise its far wider possibilities.

Dr Nathaniel Bagshaw Ward (1791–1868) did. Dr Ward was a London surgeon living in the dock area. He had tried many times to grow plants, particularly ferns, in his garden, but without success due to the smoky, sooty atmosphere of the day. The idea for what was later to be called the 'Wardian case' came to him quite by chance in 1829. His interest in plant life, and ferns in particular, was a long-standing one. He stated the following in his book *Plants in Glazed Cases* (Edition 2, 1852):

ON THE IMITATION OF THE NATURAL CONDITIONS OF PLANTS IN CLOSELY GLAZED CASES.
The science of Botany, in consequence of the perusal of the works of the immortal Linnaeus, had been my recreation from my youth up, and the earliest object of my ambition was to possess an old wall covered with ferns and mosses.

In one experiment, he was studying a moth chrysalis which he had put into a stoppered glass jar. After several days, whilst examining the chrysalis, he was surprised to see a small fern and grass growing in the jar. Dr Ward noted the moisture in the bottle and realised that the environment created was obviously that which ferns, and probably most other plants, needed to survive. They had ideal conditions – light, air, moisture and a clean atmosphere. Dr Ward kept the same glass jar, with its plants, on a window-ledge for approximately nineteen years. The plants only received fresh water once in all that time.

Dr Ward enlisted the help of a famous firm of nurserymen, Loddiges, to make up several small glass cases (greenhouses in miniature) to his own design, and he filled his London home with these. He also began to experiment with other cases and different species of plants. To test his

Fig. 2 A Wardian case of the type used by the Royal Botanical Gardens for transporting specimens until the early 1960s.

theories further, in 1833 he filled two large cases with ferns, grapes and so on and had them shipped to Sydney, Australia, where they all arrived in sound condition. In 1834 he had plants shipped back. When they were put into the case in Sydney, the temperature was 90 to 100°F (32–38°C) in the shade. Going round Cape Horn the decks were covered with a foot of snow, the temperature having dropped to around 20°F (−29°C). Nevertheless, the plants survived the eight-month journey, having been watered only once, and a new era of plant transportation had arrived.

Dr Ward realised the importance of these successful attempts to transport plants and informed Sir William J. Hooker of his findings. Sir William became the Director of Kew Gardens in 1841, and he adopted Dr Ward's method of sending and receiving plants from abroad. Among the major plants of importance to be shipped in this way were quinine, tea and rubber. Wardian cases were used by Kew Gardens to transport plants well into the 1950s, and plants were received in them by Kew until 1963. With the invention of the jet aircraft it then became possible to freight them all by air, as even the farthest countries could then be reached in a maximum of three days.

A Tiniarium planted with several varieties of succulents and cacti.

Fig. 3 (left) Reproduction of a page from the Simmer and Fleming Catalogue of 1882.

Another result of Dr Ward's discovery was the aquarium. He put forward the theory in 1836 that his cases could be suitable also for transporting from other countries some of the smaller, lower animals. He felt that if his cases gave protection to plants they could also protect living creatures. Some five years afterwards he placed several small fish into a tank of reasonable proportions, which was in a fern-house, and the fish flourished. There was no longer the necessity constantly to change the water as the aquatic plants he had in the case kept the water pure. An example of this type of case is shown in the centre of Fig. 3.

Fig. 4 Another of Dr Ward's illustrations.

Dr Ward was visited by a Mr Loudon of the *Gardener's Magazine*, at some time in 1834, specifically to see his closed cases, and he was most enthusiastic about them in his report published in the magazine. After the appearance of this article, it would seem that Dr Ward was continually asked to set his findings down on paper. Eventually, in 1842, he wrote what was to be the first edition of *Plants in Glazed Cases*. This was some twelve years after his original discovery.

Wardian cases, or terrariums as they are now known, are now used solely for decorative purposes in homes, offices, hotels etc, but in his book he writes of how 'closed cases' could benefit the poor:

ON THE APPLICATION OF THE 'CLOSED' PLAN IN IMPROVING THE CONDITION OF THE POOR.
Among the numerous useful applications of the closed cases, there is one which I believe to be of paramount importance, and well deserving the attention of every philanthropist. I mean their application to the relief of the physical and moral wants of densely crowded populations in large cities.

He goes on to state that a glazed case could be obtained relatively cheaply and that the plants to fill them could be found in the neighbouring woods of London. One such plant, still a favourite, is the common ivy. For those who could not afford the cheapest of cases, a large stoppered jar or demi-john could be used.

Fig. 5 A typical Victorian Wardian case.

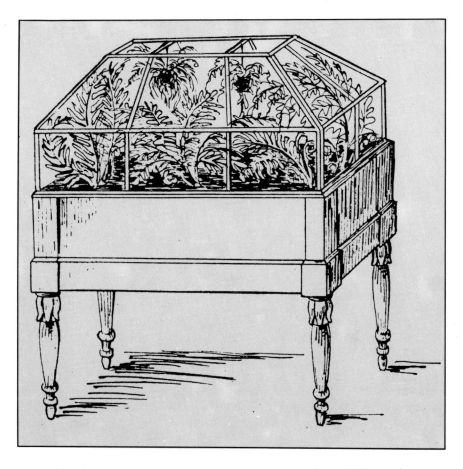

As Wardian cases grew in popularity among the middle and upper classes of Victorian society, the cases were constructed in a wide range of designs, some less attractive than others. The cases seem to have mainly contained ferns, as the Victorians had developed a passion for growing these plants. They adorned nearly all the drawing-rooms of the time, sitting inside their sometimes extremely ornate Wardian cases.

The name 'Wardian case' has now been replaced by the term 'terrarium', which comes from the Latin *terra* (earth) and -*arium* (place), and is similar to the word 'aquarium' in which *aqua* means water. Terrariums come in many different shapes and sizes, and can be easily constructed to simple designs, or be elaborate and decorative in the style of the Victorian Wardian case. Nowadays, 'terrarium' is used to describe an enclosed glass case with a door, and 'planter' to denote an open one.

2 Tools

The number of tools required to construct copperfoil terrariums and planters are really very few. Listed in this chapter are the main ones required in construction. Small, simple tools are shown in the step-by-step instructions as they are needed. The first two, the soldering iron and the glass cutter, are essential. Other tools, such as circle cutters and glass grinding machines, may be obtained as the interest in the hobby progresses.

It is always wise to buy the best quality tools available. Cheap, poor quality tools will wear out and break much more quickly, and they can also produce poor results, leading to the newcomer becoming disillusioned and losing interest.

SOLDERING IRONS

The soldering iron is one of the most expensive pieces of equipment required for constructing copperfoil projects, and it should be looked upon as an investment rather than an expense. A good quality iron will give consistently first rate results, saving time and making the hobby more worthwhile and, with luck, profitable. There are many soldering irons available, although unfortunately few are suitable for copperfoil work (see Fig. 6).

The small, low-voltage irons, used for circuit assembly, are not powerful enough to melt blowpipe solder and the tips are too narrow. Soldering guns are unsuitable as, again, the soldering tip is too narrow, and they are also rather cumbersome and heavy to handle as they have transformers incorporated into them.

Unpowered soldering irons, normally heated on a gas ring, do not retain heat long enough for bead soldering.

Large, gas-powered irons of the type sometimes used in lead light work normally get too hot, making the solder difficult to control. There is also a risk of cracking the glass with excess heat.

The ideal iron for copperfoil work should have a minimum capacity of 60 watts with either a chisel or screwdriver shaped bit, between 5–10 mm (3/16–3/8 in) across at the tip. If you cannot find a tip of exactly these dimensions, do not worry; larger size tips are quite useable, but the molten solder can be harder to control.

The iron should be able to retain sufficient heat at the tip to melt large amounts of solder used when building up a bead of solder along the joints. The temperature at the tip is important. If this is too low the solder

Fig. 6 A selection of soldering irons. Left to right: 75-watt, 100-watt temperature-controlled, 200-watt, 60-watt.

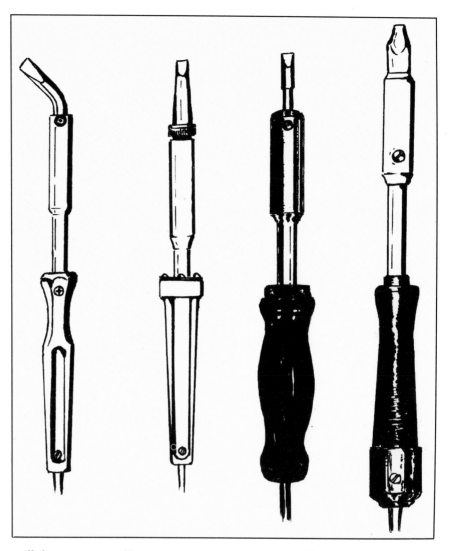

will have a crystalline, pasty appearance, it will not flow along the copperfoil and will be impossible to use. The molten solder should have a bright, shiny appearance. On the other hand, if the temperature is too high, the solder will be difficult to control. It will flow through any gaps left between the foiled pieces of glass. The ideal temperature of the soldering iron should range between 370°C (698°F) and 400°C (752°F). The maintenance of a constant temperature can be achieved in various ways.

1) Temperature-controlled Irons

As the name implies, these soldering irons are fitted with a thermostatic device, which keeps the tip at a constant temperature. Some models have interchangeable tips which have different temperature ranges. The temperature is sometimes stamped on the base of the tip. Number 7 indicates that it will obtain a temperature of 371°C (700°F), number 8 indicates a temperature of 427°C (800°F). The tips are normally iron-plated with a copper core.

2) Wattage Controllers

These provide a manual control for the soldering iron tip temperature. The ideal temperature is set by a method of trial and error: the iron should be hot enough for the solder to be bright and shiny and melt easily. Slowly increase the wattage until this is achieved. One advantage of these devices is that a number of different soldering irons can be used, but a disadvantage is that they are more suited for use with high-wattage soldering irons. Low-powered irons sometimes do not have sufficient power to overheat and so do not need to be controlled.

An inexpensive alternative is to obtain a suitable dimmer switch (make sure that the wattage of the switch is high enough for the soldering iron). Also required is a suitable three-pin socket and a box to mount the switch and the socket on. All of these can be readily obtained from electrical retailers. Constructed as shown in Fig. 7 it can make an acceptable wattage controller.

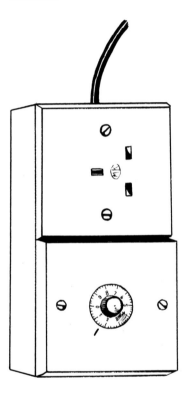

Fig. 7 Home-made wattage controller.

Most of the problems associated with soldering are due to the tip of the iron not being kept clean. It should always have a bright, shiny appearance. Because of the action of the flux and the solder, an oxide can build up on the tip which leads to a poor transfer of heat from the soldering iron tip to the solder. Wiping the tip on a wet cellulose sponge every time the iron is picked up for use will help eliminate this problem.

Always keep the tip tinned (coated with solder) at all times. If the tip does become dull and oxidised because of neglect, dip it in the flux, melt solder over the tip, re-immerse in the flux and wipe on the damp sponge. A sal ammoniac tinning block is also useful for keeping the tip shiny and bright. The soldering iron tip is worked across the block in a back and forth movement with a little solder present. In one operation the tinning block cleans and tins the tip.

Tips are normally plated with either iron or nickel to protect the copper core from the action of the flux and the solder. Iron-plated tips are normally more durable.

It is important not to file the tip as this will damage the plating and shorten the life of the tip. However, after some time in use the tip will show signs of wear. This is greatly dependent on which type of flux is used; acid flux will corrode tips quicker. When the tip does become badly corroded, filing becomes inevitable. Copper is a soft metal and can easily be filed using a fine-graded file. After filing, tin the tip using either of the methods mentioned previously. The tip will eventually need replacing. They are usually fairly inexpensive, although some of the long-life tips can be a little pricey.

The soldering iron should preferably be connected to a switched outlet so that the iron can be turned off when not in use. A plug with a neon indicator is useful as this acts as a reminder when the iron is on. Never leave the soldering iron on when not in use as this will not only cause the tip to oxidise and wear faster, but it will also become firmly attached to the iron and become harder to change. Before switching off the iron, ensure that the tip is clean and coated with solder.

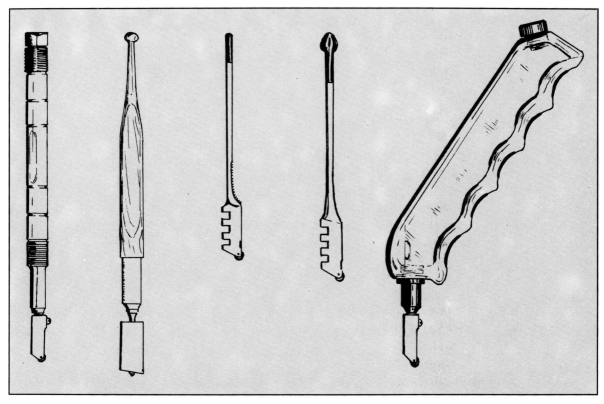

Fig. 8 A selection of glass-cutters. Left to right: self-lubricating super cutter, diamond-tipped cutter, steel wheel cutter, ball-end tungsten carbide cutter, self-lubricating hand cutter with pistol grip.

Finally, ensure that you have a safe place to rest your soldering iron when not in use. A purpose-built stand is the ideal device, and some of these have provision for a sponge to be fitted to the base. A piece of iron or steel can be useful. If the tip is rested on it the metal acts as a heat sink, helping to prevent the tip from overheating.

GLASS-CUTTING EQUIPMENT

Glass-cutting is usually the most daunting prospect for the newcomer to the hobby. Consequently, buying a good glass-cutter is an important decision. It is false economy to use an old glass-cutter that has been languishing at the bottom of a tool box for years, as it will inevitably be blunt, giving poor results.

There are a vast number of glass-cutters to choose from (see Fig. 8). They all have the same function, which is to score the surface of the glass so that it will break evenly along that score line. All glass-cutters, whether steel or tungsten carbide, need lubrication to ensure that they stay sharp and cut well. A small tin or jar with a piece of either felt or sponge placed in the bottom, soaked in a mixture of 50 per cent paraffin and 50 per cent light machine oil, will do the job perfectly.

Steel Wheel Cutters

These are the cheapest to buy. They consist of a tapered steel wheel, usually set into a die cast handle. Some models have replaceable steel wheels which clip into the handle. There are also turret models available, which have six separate wheels arranged in a turret formation. When one wheel becomes blunt the turret is slackened using a screwdriver and a fresh wheel is swivelled round into place. The turret models are only really suitable for cutting straight lines on glass. When following a curved or intricate shape marked on the glass, the thickness of the turret obscures the lines and makes them difficult to follow.

Tungsten Carbide Wheel Cutters

Similar in appearance to the single steel wheel cutter, these have a tungsten carbide wheel that will last at least ten times as long as steel if they are properly cared for. They sometimes have two or three slots at the base of the cutter, which can be used to help break the glass along the score line. Some designs of cutter have a 'ball end' on the handle. The idea is that, once the cutter has been used to score the line along the glass, the weighted ball end is used to tap the underside of the scoreline gently and make the glass easier to separate.

Self-lubricating Oil-filled Cutters

These are a significant advance on the conventional tungsten carbide wheel cutters. Oil-filled cutters, or 'super cutters' as they are sometimes called, are mostly made in Japan. They have a hollow acrylic handle which should be filled with a mixture of paraffin and light machine oil. As the steel head of the cutter is pressed down onto the glass, the oil is pumped on to a wick and lubricates the tungsten carbide wheel. The flow of the oil is controlled by adjusting the vent by means of a screw cap at the top of the cutter.

These tools normally have smaller diameter wheels than the conventional wheeled cutters; consequently, they are very useful for cutting intricate shapes. Another advantage of them is that the tungsten wheels are very hard, helpful when cutting some of the harder opalescent glass. The handle comes in two shapes: tubular, or with a pistol grip oil reservoir. The latter is very suitable for cutting long strips of glass. These cutters are the best available, but unfortunately are also expensive, being almost three times the price of an ordinary tungsten carbide cutter.

Diamond-tipped Cutter

The first method of cutting glass was by diamond-tipped tools. These have a small industrial diamond embedded in a metal head, normally attached to a wooden handle. They are not recommended for the amateur as they are awkward to use and expensive to buy.

Strip Cutters

These are normally a small turret cutter mounted onto an adjustable arm, the other end of which is attached to an L-shaped clamp which slides up and down a piece of wood screwed onto the cutting bench. There are also models which run along the edge of the glass. See Fig. 9.

Fig. 9 *Circle and strip cutters. From the top: conventional brass circle cutter, strip and circle cutter with alternative bases.*

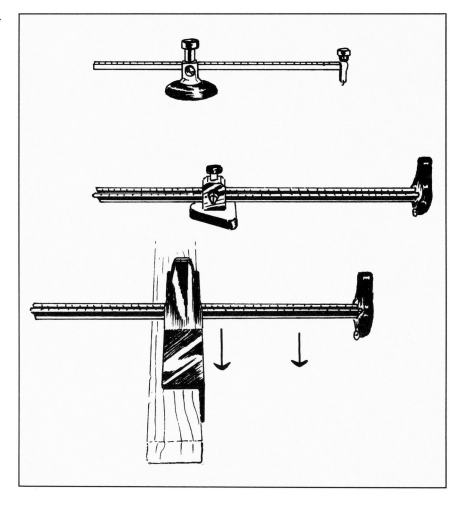

Circle Cutter

This is simply a glass cutter mounted onto an arm with a swivelling base. There are some models available which can be used as either circle or strip cutters, depending on which base is fitted. See Fig. 9.

Straight-edge

A good straight-edge is an invaluable aid to accurate glass-cutting. It can be constructed from wood, metal, perspex, or in fact anything suitable that has a perfectly straight edge. It should be at least 3 mm (⅛ in) thick so that the tip of the glass-cutter can run smoothly along the side. If using a wooden straight-edge, bear in mind that after a while the action of the cutter will cause wear and it will become inaccurate. Metal and plastic rulers have a tendency to slide across the glass. A remedy for this is to stick several thicknesses of either masking tape, felt or cork onto the underside of the ruler. Straight-edges that combine the advantages of both wood and metal are those that are designed for use with ruling pens, which are wooden rulers with a strip of metal inserted along one side. They are highly recommended if they can be obtained.

Set Square

This is useful for cutting strips of glass into accurate squares. There are several lightweight models on the market that have been specially developed for the amateur, although a small metal engineer's set square is quite adequate.

Fig. 10 Cutting-board showing various tools. Left to right: crimping device, engineering set square, wooden fid, flux brush, set square, paste brush (for brushing away glass particles).

Cutting-board

A cutting-board should be constructed from a piece of plywood, chipboard etc (see Fig. 10). Any piece of board is suitable as long as it is perfectly flat and rigid. A piece of carpet or thick felt should be stretched tightly over the surface and tacked or stapled at either end. If felt or carpet are unobtainable, a thick wad of newspapers will be sufficient to cushion the glass. If a strip cutter is to be used, a piece of 5 × 2.5 cm (2 × 1 in) wood battening should be nailed or screwed along one edge of the board. An advantage of making a cutting table is that glass-cutting can be confined to one area. As glass is scored, the small slivers of glass fly off, so keep the board clean at all times, using a small brush to clear away the slivers of waste glass. A paste brush used for paper hanging is ideal for this purpose. Never brush them away using your hands. Another advantage of the cutting-board is that it can be turned over and used for terrarium construction on the other side.

Crimping Device

This is simply a nylon block with a slot through the middle and finger grips on either side. After the piece of glass has been wrapped in foil, it is drawn through the slot and the foil is automatically pressed evenly onto the glass.

Fid

Originally, a fid was a hardwood spike used to separate strands of rope before they were to be spliced. When connected with copperfoil work, a fid is simply a piece of pointed wood used to rub down the copperfoil tape onto the glass.

Fig. 11 A selection of pliers. Left to right: traditional cut-running pliers, cut-running pliers with interchangeable jaw inserts, flared-jaw glass-breaking pliers, grozing pliers.

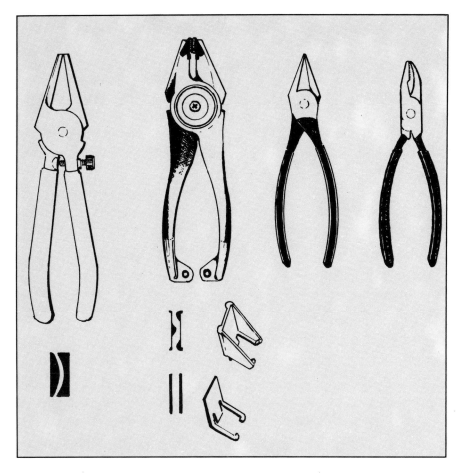

Grozing Pliers

The word 'grozing' comes from the Sanskrit, *grosdra*, which literally means 'chewing'. The use of a diamond to cut glass was only discovered in about the sixteenth century; before that date, the glass was roughly broken into the shape required with a hot iron and then laboriously chipped to its final shape with a tool called a grozing iron. Grozing pliers (see Fig. 11) are usually manufactured from drop forged steel. They have serrated edges with the lower jaw being curved. Their function is the same as in the early days of glass-cutting; they are used to chew and nibble or groze the edge of the glass to remove irregular portions once the glass has been cut.

Glass-breaking Pliers

Glass-breaking pliers (Fig. 11) are constructed so that the wide jaws are parallel when opened. They grip the edge of the glass along the score line. These pliers are particularly useful for removing thin strips of glass that are too thin to be broken by the normal methods.

Cut-running Pliers

Made from either plastic reinforced with glass fibre or drop forged steel,

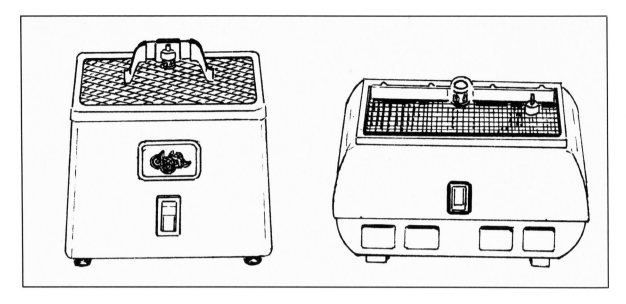

the lower jaws are convex and form an anvil for the upper concave jaw. *Fig. 12 Glass-grinding*
The even pressure that is exerted on either side of the glass causes the *machines.*
scoreline to run, hence the term 'cut-running pliers'. There are various
types of cut-running pliers on the market (Fig. 11). Some have slightly
different jaw patterns, but the principle is the same. Some models have
interchangeable jaw inserts that enable them to be converted to grozing
pliers. Cut-running pliers are helpful to break out curved glass and where
a large amount of glass-cutting is being undertaken. Due to their width
they are unsuitable for cutting very narrow slivers of glass.

GLASS-GRINDING MACHINES

There are several glass-grinding machines to choose from (see Fig. 12).
Although not a must for the beginner, they are certainly helpful for
shaping and grozing pieces of glass. The machines are of more use in the
making of Tiffany-style lampshades, where many small pieces of glass
have to fit precisely together. They consist of a motor-driven diamond-
crystal head which is water-cooled from a small reservoir inside the
machine. The water-cooling is most important, as without this facility the
head is easily damaged. The diamond crystal head revolves at approximately 3,500rpm, although some of the models can be fitted with a
footswitch to give varying speeds.

As the diamond crystals wear away, the head is moved down the shaft,
normally by means of a small grub screw on the side, and a new band of
diamond crystals are used. Various sizes and shapes of heads can be
obtained, giving different cutting patterns. Some grinders can be used to
cut bevels; others can be fitted with a flexible shaft to drive diamond-
tipped engraver's tools, a very useful accessory, if you wish to use the
methods mentioned in Chapter 4.

Most of the machines have a plastic-surfaced grinding table to avoid
scratching the glass. Grinding machines can be rather messy to operate,

The Gazebo. Maidenhair Fern (Adiantum), Begonia rex, Polka Dot Plant (Hypoestus) and a small clump of Selaginella were used for the colourful display.

A Tiniarium constructed in 2 mm glass and finished in black patina. The design is slightly modified to that mentioned in Chapter 5.

so it is best to shield them with something (a large cardboard box for instance) to avoid water splashes. One of the extras that a number of manufacturers offer is a clear plastic face-shield which is located over the diamond cutting head to avoid glass splinters being thrown up. If a face-shield is not available, it is advisable to wear a pair of industrial safety goggles to avoid the risk of flying glass particles.

COPPERFOILING MACHINES

These machines, although not essential, become very useful when a large amount of glass has to be foiled. The machines have various sizes of roller, depending on the width of foil being used. A metal peg locates the glass centrally onto the foil, and as the glass is moved the machine automatically crimps the foil around the glass at the same time as removing the backing paper from the foil. Some models have a capacity for two widths of tape. The advantage of this is that there is no need to change the roller when tape of a different width is being used. The manufacturers claim that a time saving of as much as 60 per cent over the normal hand-foiling technique can be obtained. Machines are more suitable for applying foil to square pieces of glass; small curved pieces tend to be rather more difficult and can be foiled better by hand. After removing the foiled piece, it still has to be rubbed down flat on to the surface of the glass using a wooden fid or the crimping device.

Although not as sophisticated or as quick as the shop-bought models, a foiling machine that can be made from household items is illustrated in Fig. 13. Rather 'Heath Robinson' in appearance, we can assure the reader that we have been using the machine for many years. All that is needed are the following items:

   2 steel shelf brackets (at least 15 cm [6 in]).
   1 piece of flat board (plywood, chipboard etc) measuring 25 × 50 cm
      (10 × 20).
   2 cable clamps or similar.
   1 tin lid, approximately 7.5 cm (3 in) in diameter.

Fig. 13 A home-made copperfoiling machine.

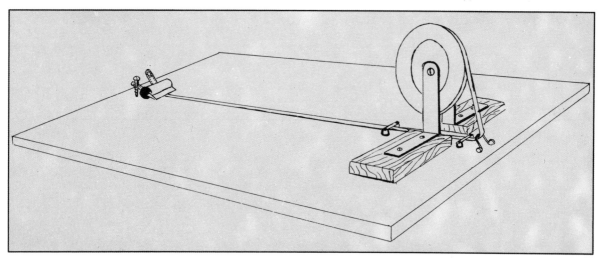

1 bulldog clip.

screws, nails etc.

Construct as shown in the drawing opposite.

To operate the foiling machine, unroll the copperfoil tape, peel the backing paper away and stretch the foil into the bulldog clip; peel the remaining backing paper away, place the glass centrally on the tape and wrap the foil around the remaining edges of the glass, lightly crimping the foil onto the glass as you go. Remember to allow a 6 mm (¼ in) overlap of foil. Cut the foil with a craft knife and finally smooth the foil onto the glass using either a fid or a crimping device.

3 Materials

Most of the materials used in the construction of copperfoil terrariums should be easy to obtain from local sources. Suitable solder and certain fluxes can be bought from plumbers' merchants and large engineering supply companies. The latter are also useful places to look for soldering irons, glass-cutters and pliers etc. Glass merchants can obviously supply clear and mirrored glass but, if approached tactfully, many are very willing to impart knowledge. If an interest in glass is shown they can be a fund of information on how to cut and handle glass correctly. Coloured glass may be harder to obtain, although with the renewed interest in lead light windows and stained glass in general many glass merchants now carry a limited stock.

Copper sulphate and other chemicals used for making the various patinas are obtained from either chemists or chemical suppliers. Unfortunately, however, chemical suppliers are sometimes only willing to supply in larger quantities.

Copperfoil tape can be a difficult item to find. Some craft shops sell it but these seem to be few and far between. The best sources can be found in the list of suppliers in the Appendix. Many operate a fast, efficient mail-order service. They can also be useful for obtaining the items of glass, solder, tools etc that may not be found locally.

GLASS

Most flat, clear glass produced today is manufactured from the same basic materials and formulation that has been used for thousands of years. It was under the Roman Empire that regular production of transparent and nearly colourless glass was achieved, although the making of glass by fusion can be traced back to the Phoenicians.

Most clear window glass is produced by heating silica (sand), soda and lime together at a temperature of over 1500°C (2732°F). Clear glass, which is known as soda lime glass, consists of 73 per cent silica sand, the basic raw material, with 14 per cent soda, 9 per cent lime and 4 per cent magnesia. Silica itself needs a very high temperature (1900°C/3452°F) to melt it, but by adding the soda the melting temperature is almost halved. Unfortunately, this formulation produces a glass which is soluble in water and is known as waterglass. However, by adding limestone as a stabiliser, a very durable non-soluble glass is produced. Scrap glass, known as cullett, is also added to the mixture as this assists in the melting process. When the ingredients have been heated together they form a viscous

The Victorian—an ideal structure for tall plants.

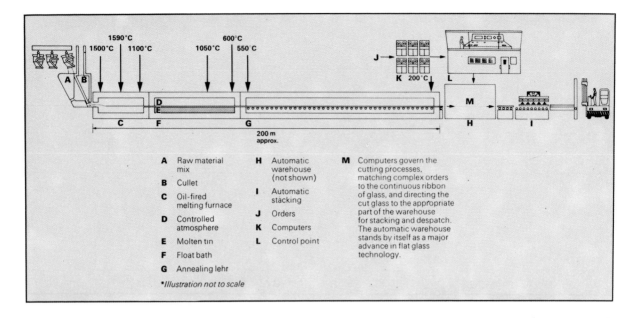

A Raw material mix

B Cullet

C Oil-fired melting furnace

D Controlled atmosphere

E Molten tin

F Float bath

G Annealing lehr

H Automatic warehouse (not shown)

I Automatic stacking

J Orders

K Computers

L Control point

M Computers govern the cutting processes, matching complex orders to the continuous ribbon of glass, and directing the cut glass to the appropriate part of the warehouse for stacking and despatch. The automatic warehouse stands by itself as a major advance in flat glass technology.

*Illustration not to scale

liquid with an appearance similar to that of treacle. As the mixture cools, the viscosity increases and eventually the glass becomes hard. The controlled cooling of glass is very important; if the glass is cooled too rapidly it does not have time to release the stresses that can build up within it, resulting in the glass sometimes breaking at room temperature. By carefully monitoring the rate at which glass cools down, these stresses are released. This results in a piece of glass that is easy to handle. The cooling process is known as annealing.

Fig. 14 · The float glass process.

Float Glass

Nearly all clear glass available throughout the world is produced by the float glass process (see Fig. 14), invented in 1952 by Alistair Pilkington of Pilkington Brothers, the world-renowned glass-makers. Float glass was a revolutionary step in glass-making, as it was an entirely different process from any that had been used before. It took seven years and £7 million to develop. Over 102,000 tonnes (100,000 tons) of waste glass was produced before the first saleable glass was made in 1959.

The process makes use of a furnace which is continually fed with raw materials. After the ingredients have been melted, the ribbon of molten glass flows from the furnace on to a large bath of molten tin. This is the heart of the process. The bath is enclosed in a controlled atmosphere to prevent the tin from oxidising. The ribbon of glass floating on the tin is held at a sufficiently high temperature for long enough to allow the surface of the glass to become perfectly smooth. The ribbon of glass is then gradually cooled as it progresses across the molten tin, until it is cool enough to enter the annealing lehr (oven). The glass continues through the lehr, cooling slowly, to reduce the stresses in the finished glass which will make it easy to cut.

The finished glass emerges from the lehr at a temperature of 200°C

(392°F). The cutting of the finished glass is controlled by a computer which matches the orders for glass to the continuous stream of glass being produced. The glass is finally taken off the end of the line by overhead cranes fitted with suckers. The finished glass is stored in a computer-controlled warehouse.

The final product is used for many things such as car windscreens, double glazing, bandit-proof windows, plus of course most forms of ordinary glazing. Float glass is manufactured in thicknesses of between 2 mm and 25 mm. The most suitable thicknesses for terrarium construction are those between 2 mm and 4 mm. Using 2 mm glass produces narrow solder joints which give the finished structure a delicate appearance. Thin glass obviously weighs less and this can be an important factor when making larger projects. The main disadvantage with thin glass is that it can easily crack if molten solder is dropped onto it.

There is nothing more disheartening than to be nearing completion of a terrarium and have the glass crack as the last bead of solder is being applied. This problem can be alleviated by remembering to place a piece of rag under the joint that is being soldered.

Another problem with 2 mm glass is that a lot of glass merchants do not stock it, as demand is generally low; 3 mm glass is far easier to obtain. Although the finished terrarium does not have such a delicate look, it does have the advantage of being less likely to crack if the molten solder should be dropped onto it. 3 mm glass is also sometimes easier to cut than thinner glass. Most of the models illustrated in colour were constructed using 3 mm glass.

Using 4 mm glass in construction should be avoided if at all possible. The finished terrarium will have thicker solder joints, and on larger projects the weight of the glass can cause problems when assembly is being undertaken. Also, the thicker glass tends to be harder to cut, especially when grozing or removing thin slivers of glass from the edges. 4 mm glass is best left for making the bases of terrariums.

Mirrored Glass

Mirrored glass is ordinary float glass that has had a silver nitrate solution chemically sprayed on to it. The silvering is protected from oxidation by having a paint-like substance coated onto it after manufacture. Mirrored glass is available in thicknesses ranging from 2 mm to 6 mm. The same rules apply as for cutting float glass: always remember to cut the mirror on the reflective side, and keep the workbench completely free from glass slivers when cutting mirrored glass, as these can easily scratch and spoil the silvering.

When constructing a terrarium with a mirror back, do not let the flux come into contact with the back, as some fluxes can penetrate the protective coating and damage the silvering.

Drawn Flat Glass

Vertical drawn glass is a method of producing clear, flat glass, still used in many Eastern Bloc and developing countries today. It is also used by some manufacturers in Europe for producing stained glass. There are a number of variations but the principle is the same.

The molten glass is produced in a large tank furnace. At the start of glass production, a webbed metal frame called a bait is lowered into the molten glass. As it is raised out of the tank, the molten glass is manually teased until it is gripped by knurled water-cooled rollers that are positioned on either side of an annealing tower. The purpose of these rollers is to achieve a uniform thickness and to prevent the glass 'wasting'. The ribbon of glass is fed slowly up through the tower which is approximately 9.5 m (31 ft) high, between asbestos-covered powered rollers. At the top of the tower the bait is removed and the ribbon of glass is then drawn up the tower in a continuous stream. As the finished glass reaches the top of the tower, the glass is cut into stock sizes and stored.

Drawn glass has a hard, fire-polished surface, similar in many ways to float glass. Due to its method of production, however, some distortion caused by the rollers occasionally appears as streaks and bubbles in the glass.

Most horticultural glass is produced by the drawn glass process. Although used mainly for glazing greenhouses, it is an ideal material for building terrariums – after all, they are miniature greenhouses. Horticultural glass is easy to obtain from many glass merchants. It is 3 mm thick and extremely cheap. The slight distortion in the glass can lend character to the finished item. Horticultural glass has the same cutting characteristics as float glass, but, being a lot cheaper, it is a perfect material to practise glass-cutting with.

Mouthblown Glass

Blown glass is produced by the cylinder or broad glass method (see Fig. 15). It is believed to date back to the Romans who used this method from about A.D. 45 to produce early window glass. When the Crystal Palace was erected on its original site in Hyde Park in 1851, almost a million square feet of hand-blown cylinder glass was produced in six months by Chance Brothers of Birmingham.

Because of the very nature of the process, each sheet of glass has its own character regarding colour effects, surface texture and variations in thickness and finish. Consequently, no two sheets are exactly alike. Many of the techniques and formulations used to achieve certain types of glass are closely-guarded secrets, being handed down over many years.

Batches of raw materials are first carefully measured and mixed together. The basic materials are silica sand, soda and limestone. These are mixed with metal oxides to give the glass its various colours. Cobalt oxide produces a blue glass and ferrous oxide green; carbon and sulphur compound is added to achieve an amber glass, and so on. The materials are melted in a small fireclay furnace. A gather of molten, clear glass is taken from a separate furnace onto the blowpipe, and on top of this is taken a gather of coloured glass from the first furnace; these are then

Fig. 15 The cylinder method of mouthblown glass making.

mixed together to produce the final coloured glass. The gather is shaped in a hollow wooden block which is lubricated with beeswax. The mixed and shaped gather is returned to the furnace and another gather of clear glass is made. This third gather is not mixed with the first two, as the finished glass will be a layer of clear glass adhering to a layer of mixed clear and coloured glass.

The three gathers are then returned to the wooden block for final

31

shaping. The correct shaping of the molten glass is important as it helps to maintain uniform thickness of the glass as it is blown. Being very thick at this stage the first inflation is made using compressed air. The glass then has to be re-heated to make it workable again. The blowpipe is swung to and fro to make the bubble of glass into an elongated sphere. The neck of the bubble further away from the blowpipe is marked using a large pair of metal tweezers. By blowing cold air onto this mark, the neck of the bubble can be broken off, leaving a hole at the end of the bubble. The bubble of glass is again re-heated, and the hole is then opened up by rotating the bubble of glass first one way and then the other on a former which has been sprinkled with sawdust.

This carbonises, and acts as a lubricant so that the glass does not become marked while being shaped. A stick is inserted in the end of the bubble and is used to open out the hole and help form the bubble into a cylindrical shape. A solid metal rod with a disc of glass at the end, called a punty, is then fused onto the opened-out end of the cylinder. The blowpipe is then removed. The glass is again re-heated and the other end of the cylinder is opened out using a similar method. The punty is then removed and the completed muffs are placed in an annealing lehr to be slowly cooled.

After the muffs have completely cooled, they are split longitudinally, ready for the flattening process. The muffs are placed in a special kiln which heats them to a temperature at which the glass begins to soften. As they reach this temperature, they are carefully manipulated on to the flattening stone. They are manoeuvred with an iron rod so that the split is at the top of the cylinder. This is to avoid the cylinder falling in on itself. The muff slowly begins to unfold under its own weight, and is finally flattened by rubbing a wooden block attached to a metal pole over the muff. The wood carbonises on the hot glass and acts as a lubricant to ensure that the glass is not scratched and has a good fire-finished surface. The flattened glass is then annealed, inspected and cut to size.

Due to the manufacturing process of mouthblown glass, the thickness of the finished product can vary considerably.

Rolled Glass

Much of the stained and patterned glass that is produced today is manufactured by the rolled glass method. This was invented by James Hartley of Sunderland, an early pioneer in glass-making, who in 1847 simply ladled molten glass from the founding pot on to the stone cooling table and then rolled it to produce relatively thin, translucent pieces of glass about 3 mm thick. The process was developed under licence from Hartley by Pilkingtons, and in the 1880s patterned or figured rolled glass was beginning to be produced. This was achieved by cutting simple patterns onto the stone casting table on which the glass was rolled.

In 1884 a pair of blacksmiths, Frederick Mason and John Conqueror, invented a machine where molten glass was poured onto an inclined plate and passed between a pair of iron rollers to obtain an even thickness. Chance Brothers, who were a large glass-making company in Birmingham, found that, by adding a second pair of rollers and engraving a pattern on the lower one, a patterned glass could be produced. This was the basis on which all modern machine-rolled glass is produced. Nowadays a continuous ribbon of glass passes between two horizontal water-cooled rollers. The distance that they are set apart determines the thickness of the finished glass. The bottom roller has the pattern either embossed or engraved onto it. After rolling, the ribbon of glass passes slowly over a number of powered rollers through a long, horizontal annealing lehr.

Because of its versatility many different types of glass can be produced. Wired glass, which was first produced in 1898 to meet new safety regulations for the use of glass in skylights and firedoors, is produced using a modified version of the rolled glass method. Many different colours and patterns of stained glass can be produced using the method.

Although regarded by some purists as not having such depth and movement of colour, rolled glass has many of the characteristics of traditional mouthblown antique stained glass. Rolled glass normally has a uniform thickness range of about 2.5 mm to 4 mm depending on the manufacturers and pattern. Being of an even thickness it is ideal for copperfoil projects.

Types of Stained and Coloured Glasses

Cathedral Glass

Cathedral is a very old term which was originally used to describe a certain type of patterned, translucent, machine-made coloured glass. Nowadays it is a name used for any translucent, machine-made glass which has a pattern on one side and is smooth on the other. Cathedral glass is normally the easiest coloured glass to obtain, is fairly inexpensive to buy and is generally as easy to cut as clear glass.

Antique Glass

Antique glass means that it has been produced by the mouthblown cylinder process that has been used for thousands of years. The word 'antique' relates to the method of glass-making and has nothing to do with the age of the glass. Many stained glass studios will use nothing but antique glass due to its unique characteristics. The glass has a beautiful crystalline surface with hundreds of tiny surface lines that give it a finish all of its own.

There are many variations of antique glass. Hartley Wood, the famous English antique glass-makers, alone produce over 300 different types and shades of antique glass. Due to the way it is manufactured, antique glass has a varying overall thickness making it sometimes difficult to incorporate in copperfoil projects. If being used for terrarium construction, it is best to choose the glass carefully and try to find pieces that have a uniform thickness, as these are easier to cut.

Semi-antique Glass

This is a term often used to describe machine-rolled glass which has been made with some of the features found in antique glass.

Opalescent Glass

Opalescent glass is opaque, and is a mixture of white glass with streaks of two or three colours in the body of the sheet. Opalescent glass is machine-made and has an even thickness. It is very useful in terrarium construction where the opaque glass can be used for the lower parts to hide the root structure and compost. Opaque glass should be used sparingly as too much will block out the natural light to the growing plants. Opalescent glass is normally easy to cut, although some of them which contain more white and red colours do require a sharp carbide cutter.

Art Glass

This is a term used mostly by American glass-makers. It is used to describe a machine-made glass that has some special feature such as a pattern embossed on the glass or a textured finish.

Water Glass

This is a glass with a surface texture that gives a water-like appearance. It is not to be confused with the early water-soluble glass produced by melting silica sand, soda and lime together.

Wispy Glass

Wispy glass is a mixture of opalescent and cathedral resulting in a glass that is more translucent than opaque. It is a machine-rolled glass of an even thickness, very useful for adding colour to copperfoil projects.

Glue Chip Glass

Glue chip glass is normally a cathedral glass that has been sand-blasted. A thin layer of animal glue is applied and the glass is then heated in an oven until the glue hardens, which causes the surface of the glass to flake off, resulting in a beautiful random fern-like pattern in the finished glass.

Fractures and Streamers

Fractures are small thin pieces of glass rather like confetti. Streamers are long thin strings of molten glass, rather reminiscent of thin cake icing. Both are laid on the casting table before the molten glass is poured over them. The fractures and streamers become fused with the molten glass leaving a unique three-dimensional foliage pattern in the finished glass.

Iridescent Glass

Light reflected from the surface of the glass reveals the iridescent finish, and light passing through it shows the colour of the glass underneath. When used on opal glass the glass is given a mother-of-pearl effect. On translucent glass, the effect is similar to oil floating on water.

A Petal Planter with a pleasing combination of house plants and cut flowers. The effect was achieved by placing a small jar with a piece of oasis in the bottom of the planter and covering it with the compost.

Flashed Glass

This is antique glass that has a second layer of colour applied to one side of the glass. All flashed glass is best cut on the side opposite to the flashing.

Smooth Glass

This is coloured glass that is smooth and untextured, similar to float glass.

Hammered, Ripple and Granite

This is a heavy texture rolled on one side of the glass, often found in cathedral glass.

Reamy Glass

Reams were originally imperfections such as lines, bumps and bubbles which were left in the glass to show that it had been mouthblown. However, today a number of companies produce machine-made reamy glass, every sheet being different.

Seedy Glass

Seedy glass has minute bubbles trapped in the glass giving a fizzy drink or raindrop look to it.

Pot Colour Glass

This is a single-coloured antique glass, with the glass a uniform colour throughout.

Crackle Glass

This has a large crackle pattern, which has a similar effect to broken glass.

COPPERFOIL

Copperfoil is a thin ductile tape made from almost pure copper (see Fig. 16). It is backed with a specially-formulated pressure-sensitive acrylic adhesive, which is designed to withstand high temperatures. The backing paper is peeled off and the tape is wrapped around the glass forming a C shape. The copperfoil acts as a membrane over which the molten solder flows, for constructing the terrarium or planter.

Copperfoil is available in different thicknesses ranging from 0.001 in (one thou.) up to 0.0015 in (one and a half thou.). Thicker foils are made but they are normally unsuitable for copperfoil work. The choice of foil is very much dependent on individual preference and availability. Thinner foil is easier to fold round the glass and less tiring on the fingers. It should however be applied with care as it can tear on the sharp edges and corners of the glass. Thicker foil is more durable but can be rather more exhausting, especially when a large amount of foiling has to be done and burnished by hand. As stated, it really is a matter of choice and availability. Copperfoil is only manufactured in Imperial widths which range from 5/32 in (4 mm) up to about ½ in (13 mm).

Widths of Copperfoil Tape

5/32 in (4 mm)

This width can be used for foiling 2 mm glass. It has to be applied with care to ensure an even overlap on either side. The result is a structure with very fine solder lines and a very delicate appearance. It is not really suitable for larger, heavier structures.

3/16 in (4.75 mm)

This width is widely used with 2 mm glass. Application does not have to be as accurate as with the 5/32 in foil, and there is some room for error if the glass is not quite central on the foil. Although the finished solder joints do not have such a delicate look, the final structure is far more robust.

7/32 in (5.5 mm)

Foil of this width is used on 3 mm glass where a fairly thin solder joint is required. As with the 5/32 in foil on 2 mm glass, the foil has to be applied accurately.

1/4 in (6.25 mm)

The ideal width for foiling 4 mm glass, this can be applied without trouble and any inaccuracy is easily covered up. Many newcomers to the hobby start with 1/4 in foil and progress to 7/32 in as their foiling becomes more accurate.

5/16 in (8 mm)

This can be used to make projects in 4 mm glass. It is not recommended, as the finished article has large solder joints and a rather clumsy appearance. 5/16 in and the wider foils are generally used in the areas where strength is required, such as attaching hinges to door surrounds and where latches are mounted, for example.

Copperfoil Squares

Copperfoil squares are made from the same material as the foil, although sometimes they are a little thicker. They come in various sizes, but 12 × 12 in (30 × 30 cm) seems to be one of the most popular. The squares are very useful for cutting filigree patterns and then coating them with solder.

SOLDER

Solder is an alloy of tin and lead. The melting point of solder depends on the percentage of the two metals used. Tin melts at 232°C (450°F) and lead melts at 327°C (621°F). However, when the two are combined the melting point can be lowered to as little as 183°C (361°F). The table overleaf illustrates the melting points of the various alloys.

As the amount of tin content is increased and the lead reduced from the 63/37 combination, the melting point begins to increase again until at

Tin (%)	Lead (%)	Melting point
0	100	327°C (621°F)
10	90	300°C (572°F)
30	70	258°C (496°F)
40	60	238°C (460°F)
50	50	216°C (421°F)
60	40	190°C (375°F)
63	37	183°C (361°F)*

*This is the lowest melting point of the alloy.

100 per cent tin, the melting point has reached 232°C (450°F). The most common solder available is called solid-cored blowpipe solder. It contains 40 per cent tin and 60 per cent lead. It is sold either in small reels or, more commonly, in sticks about 4.75 mm (3/16 in) wide and 60 cm (2 ft) long. In this form it is normally sold by weight. There are approximately 14 to 15 sticks in 1 kg (2.2 lb).

Solders with different percentages of alloys are made. Solder with 60 per cent tin and 40 per cent lead can be obtained. This has the advantage of being easier to use for obtaining even beads of solder. Having a lower melting temperature it can respond better to a cooler iron which can be an advantage when building large structures. Its great disadvantage is that due to the high tin content it is rather expensive, almost twice as costly as conventional blowpipe solder.

A compromise which some craft outlets are beginning to sell is solder

Fig. 16 Solder, fluxes, patinas and copperfoil tape.

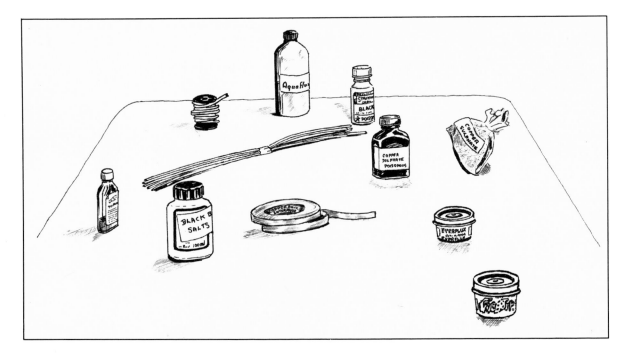

with a 50 per cent tin and 50 per cent lead content. It has a lower melting point than blowpipe solder, yet is still cheaper than the 60/40 variety. Another advantage of this solder, if it can be obtained, is that it is supplied with a special cored water-soluble flux, thus eliminating the need for separate flux application. This solder should not be confused with conventional multi-core resin solder that is used for electrical work. Resin-cored solder is not suitable for copperfoil work as the resin flux is very hard to remove from the glass. It would also be astronomically expensive if used on even the smallest planter.

Solder is the most expensive of the materials used in terrarium construction (see Fig. 16), although some of the more exotic pieces of stained glass can come a close second. Large amounts of solder are used on three-dimensional copperfoil items such as terrariums and planters, as the solder first has to fill in the gaps left between the individual pieces of glass, on top of which a bead of solder has to be made. The price of solder often varies considerably due to the fluctuations in the world metal markets but buying in bulk can attract discounts.

FLUXES

Flux is a substance which must be applied to the copperfoil before soldering commences, to help promote the fusion of the solder with the metal. The flux removes the oxides from the surface of the copper which have formed by exposure to the atmosphere. Flux helps to make the molten solder flow easily along the joints, making an even bead of solder easier to form.

There are many types and formulations of flux available in paste, gel and liquid form (see Fig. 16). Some of the leading commercial fluxes, especially those sold by plumbers' merchants, have a high acid content which can give off unpleasant fumes and can corrode the tips of soldering irons quickly. They are often known as active fluxes. Their one great advantage is that they clean the copperfoil extremely well and help to promote a good solder joint.

Over the past few years some manufacturers have developed fluxes that do not contain acid. They are frequently promoted by showing that they can be applied by the fingertip instead of by brush. Although not as fierce as acid fluxes, the fumes are not as obnoxious and soldering iron tips obviously last longer.

Some of the specialised companies who supply the copperfoil hobbyist supply water-soluble fluxes. These do not release unpleasant fumes, but they must normally be re-applied if the solder joint has to be re-worked. This kind of flux is very economical as they are normally diluted 50/50 with water. Liquid flux tends to boil under the molten solder if applied too liberally, causing it to spatter with a very displeasing effect. Mirror flux is a special flux formulated so that it will not harm the silvering on the back of mirrors.

Any flux is best applied with either a small, stiff brush or a flux applicator. This is simply a piece of sponge on a handle. Either device will make flux application more economical and ensure that the flux is worked into any awkward gaps left between the copperfoiled pieces. If available a paste flux is preferable to a liquid as it does not have the tendency to flow away.

PATINAS

Various patinas can be applied to give different finishes to the completed terrarium or planter (see Fig. 16).

Copper Sulphate

This is the chemical most used for darkening solder and giving the finished terrarium a copper-coloured antique look. The depth of colour is dependent on the amount of copper sulphate used. This can range from a light copper finish to a dark bronze. Copper sulphate is usually supplied in crystal form and has to be mixed with hot water before it will dissolve. There are probably as many different methods of mixing and applying this material as there are craftsmen using it, and some of these methods are described in Chapter 4. Be warned copper sulphate is poisonous.

Black Patina

Normally supplied in a ready-mixed form, this solution contains nitric acid and selenium dioxide. When applied to freshly-cleaned solder it turns it to a very dark grey, almost black colour. This patina should be applied using extreme care.

Black Bronzing Salts

This is a patina that when applied to brass gives it an attractive antique type finish which blends well with the solder that has been stained with a copper sulphate solution. Supplied in granular form it is mixed with cloudy household ammonia. This solution can be a little unpleasant and is best applied in a well-ventilated room. The depth of the antique finish depends upon how long the brass items are submerged in the mixture. After approximately five minutes, the item should be removed from the liquid and rinsed under running water. It can be very useful for removing the bright, shiny finish from brass finials, hinges and channelling used for making doors etc.

4 Construction Methods

The two skills that have to be mastered for the successful construction of copperfoil terrariums and planters are the ability firstly to cut glass accurately, and secondly to apply a neat, well-rounded bead of solder with not too many lumps and bumps along it. Neither of these is hard to achieve if a little perseverance and common sense are used. Even if, as the first project is taking shape, it is perhaps not going together quite as planned, it is well worth completing as the end result can often be a pleasant surprise.

All of the projects described in Chapter 5 are designed for ease of construction. The basis of building is the same in all cases, although for some it has to be modified a little. The dimensions mentioned should be regarded as a guide only, as they can be made larger or smaller to suit

Fig. 17 Drawing the template.

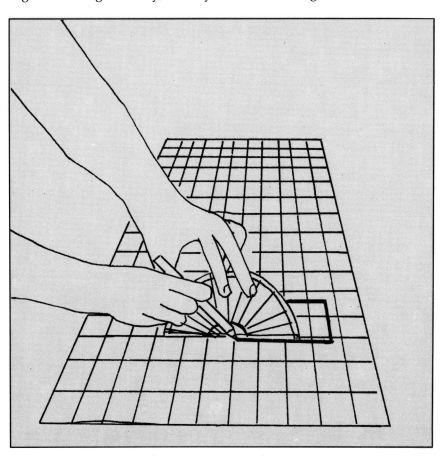

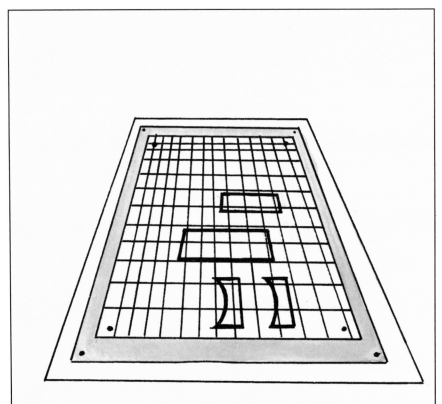

Fig. 18 Making the template.

individual requirements. All of the models illustrated in colour in this book were built to the dimensions given in Chapter 5. If making a terrarium or planter to your own design, it is often a good idea to construct it first using thick cardboard, sticking it together with masking tape. This not only gives some indication of the size of the finished structure, but it can also show up any difficulties that may be encountered in the making of it. Mostly, of course, it saves time and money. The most important factor for successful construction is accuracy, especially in the drawing and making of the templates and the cutting of the glass.

The Mirrorback model has been chosen to illustrate the stages of construction as it covers all of the various skills that have to be mastered.

MAKING TEMPLATES

Take a sheet of graph paper (preferably with metric squares), and with a ruler and ballpen draw the shape of the template using the dimensions mentioned in Chapter 5 (see Fig. 17). If modifying the measurements remember to increase or decrease all of the relevant ones by the same amount. For instance, it is of no use widening section B without increasing the width of sections A and C where they join it. The advantage of using graph paper is that it ensures that all of the templates are as accurate as possible. When drawing angles it is best to check these by using a protractor.

The templates can be made from any kind of stiff material. Most types

(Opposite) A Mirrorback constructed using seedy glass for the top section and with two side panels omitted to allow room for the dried flower arrangement. The base section has etched glass to help obscure the oasis. Flowers used in this arrangement include Quaking Grass (Briza), Chinese Lanterns (Physalis), Honesty (Lunaria), Helichrysum, Glycerined Beech (Fagus), Scabious (Scabiosa) seedheads, and pods of Iris sibirica.

of cardboard are suitable as long as they are perfectly flat. Manilla folders, of the type found in offices, are quite useable; their only fault is that they wear quickly. Thin aluminium or styrene sheets are useful. These can be obtained in various thicknesses from model or hobby shops and are very easy to cut and extremely durable.

Place the material chosen onto a flat surface and lay down a sheet or sheets of carbon transfer paper (carbonised side down) large enough to cover the surface of the template material (see Fig. 18). Next, place the template drawing on top of these two and by using either sticky tape or drawing pins (not a good idea if using the dining-room table!) ensure that the template material and the drawing are securely fastened together and cannot be moved in relation to each other. Take the ruler and pen and trace the lines from the top copy, being sure to use sufficient pressure to transfer the design through onto the medium underneath. Trace the complete design and then separate the sheets. If the template design needs to be preserved for future projects, simply lay a piece of tracing or greaseproof paper over it before commencing to draw the template.

With a sharp knife (a small craft knife or a scalpel are ideal) and a ruler, carefully cut the template. Try to ensure that the cut is as exactly on the drawn line as possible. If using styrene or aluminium, score along the line two or three times and then bend the metal or plastic up and down until it parts. If cutting templates where angles are involved, check them after cutting by tracing round the design on to a piece of plain paper and then simply turning the template over and laying it back over the outline, to ensure that the angles are the same. An accurate set of templates will make for easier construction later on.

CUTTING THE GLASS

Before the glass is marked for cutting, it is best if it has already been cut into strips of the correct width by the glass merchants. This has two

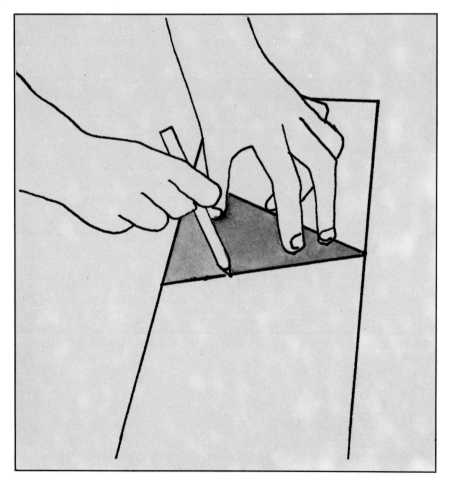

Fig. 19 Marking the glass.

Fig. 20 Cutting the glass.

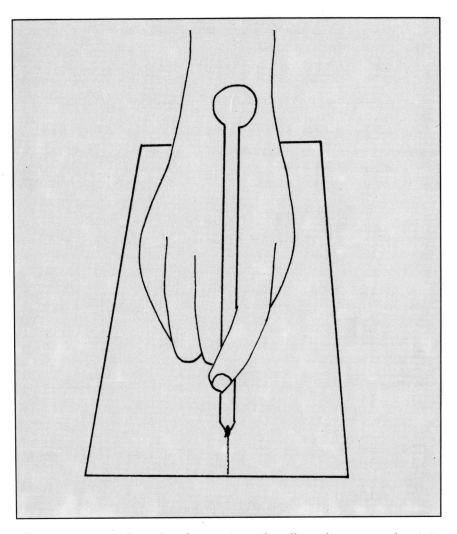

advantages: not only is the glass easier to handle and transport, but it is also more economical to use with less waste. Place the glass on the cutting table if one has been made, or, if not, spread several thicknesses of newspaper to cushion the work surface. Remember to treat all glass with care, and wear gloves if necessary. Slide a piece of white paper under the glass; this will help to make the lines marked on the glass easier to see. Ensure that the glass is thoroughly clean and free from greasy marks; polish with a lint-free cloth if in doubt. Place the template on the glass and trace the design onto the glass using either a spirit-based felt-tip pen, with as fine a point as possible, or an ordinary ballpoint pen. Make sure that the template does not move while the design is being traced (see Fig. 19).

Before cutting the glass that has been so carefully marked, it is best to practise on some scrap pieces until glass can be cut without any problem.

When cutting and grozing glass, small slivers can fly up and be dangerous. It is therefore advisable for non-spectacle wearers to obtain a pair of plastic safety glasses to protect their eyes from the flying particles.

The object of cutting glass is to score lightly and break the surface of the

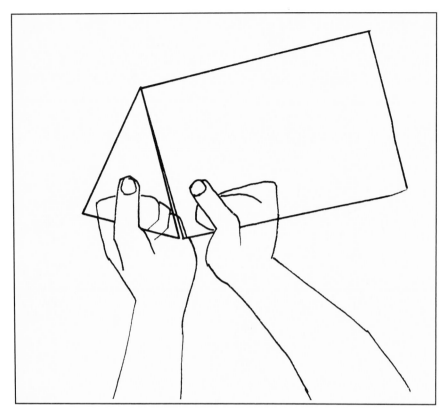

Fig. 21 Breaking the glass using the downward twisting movement of the wrists.

glass with the wheel of the cutter. After this, by applying even pressure to either side of the scoreline, the glass will part. There are no hard and fast rules as to how to hold the glass-cutter; it is really up to the individual to find a grip that is most comfortable. Many find that holding it in a similar fashion to a pen gives satisfactory results. Others prefer to hold the cutter further up the handle to obtain more leverage.

The glass to be cut should be perfectly clean. The cutter will work more efficiently if it has been lubricated with a machine oil/paraffin mixture. This not only helps to make the cut easier, but it also keeps the cutting wheel sharp. Place the cutter on the edge of the glass furthest away from you and, using the straight edge or set square as a guide, pull the cutter towards you in one easy movement (see Fig. 20). The object of the exercise is to maintain an even pressure right through the cutting stroke. When glass-cutting is first attempted, there is often a tendency to be heavy-handed and overscore the glass. This is apparent if, after the glass has been cut, the scoreline pops and splinters. Never go over a scoreline twice, as this will not only blunt the cutting wheel but it will also make the glass even harder to break. Try to avoid going off the edge of the glass at the end of the cutting stroke as this can also dull the cutting wheel. The secret to successful glass-cutting is to perfect moving the cutter down, using even pressure throughout the cutting stroke. After some practice the correct sound of the glass-cutter scoring the glass will become apparent.

Fig. 22 Tapping the glass underneath the scoreline.

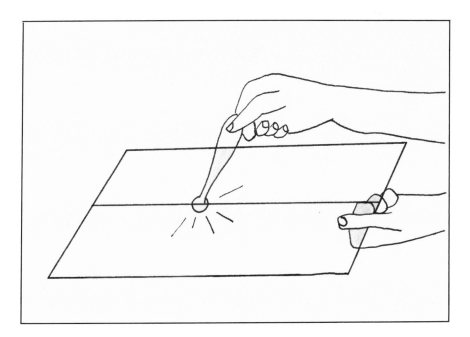

Mirrored Glass

Mirrored glass is basically float glass that has had a silvered finish applied, and so can be cut in the same way as ordinary glass. It should always be cut on the reflective side, not on the side that has been coated. Remember to keep the work bench clear of glass slivers as they can mark the silvering.

Stained Glass

When cutting stained glass, it is best with some of them to practise cutting on either side to establish which is the easiest. This is especially true when cutting various types of opalescent glass. Having gained sufficient practice in glass-cutting, the glass that has been marked can now be cut. Place the straight-edge along the line, allowing a sufficient gap for the off-set of the cutter wheel. Place the cutter on the glass, ensuring that the wheel follows the marked line exactly. With an even pressure score the line. After scoring, break the glass by one of the methods described, then re-position the template, mark the glass and score it again.

Breaking the Glass

There are several methods of breaking glass once it has been scored. The most straightforward and widely used is to grip the glass firmly in both hands either side of the scoreline, and with a positive downward twisting movement of the wrists virtually twist and pull the glass apart (see Fig. 21). This method is particularly suitable for separating 2 mm and 3 mm glass, where there is sufficient glass to grip.

If this approach seems a little ambitious, glass can be broken by placing a pencil or matchstick under the glass, along the scoreline and then pressing the two edges down until they part.

Cut-running pliers are useful when breaking sheets of glass. Simply place the scoreline over the anvil in the centre of the pliers and then press the jaws together.

Glass can also be broken by placing the scoreline along the edge of a table and bending the overhanging portion of the glass down, either by hand or, if only a thin sliver of glass exists, with glass-breaking pliers. Tapping the glass firmly underneath the scoreline until it begins to 'run', with a ball-end cutter, is very useful (see Fig. 22). This method is often used for hard-to-cut glass such as opalescent and some types of mirrored glass where awkward shapes have been cut. As the glass is tapped, the note can be heard to change as it begins to break and 'run'. It generally has a duller tone.

Narrow pieces of glass can be removed by using the notches that are cut in the side of certain glass-cutters or by using glass-breaking pliers. If the glass that has been cut has some irregularities, these can be nibbled away with grozing pliers and smoothed down with a silicon carbide stone. If grozing pliers are not available, ordinary household pliers may be used.

Awkward Shapes

If awkward and irregular shapes are to be cut, it is best to work out a sequence of cuts to obtain the desired pattern. Always cut the shape away from the main sheet. This helps to prevent one of the cuts running and ruining the complete sheet. Avoid designing shapes which have internal right angles, as these are nearly impossible to cut. When marking out the glass, always allow for some waste. Leave sufficient spare glass around the glass being cut to allow the scorelines to be gripped with either pliers or fingers.

Cutting Semi-circles

To cut the attractive semi-circular pieces of glass used in many of the models illustrated in this book, all that is required is a circle cutter mounted on a flat piece of board. A simple jig arrangement is laid out on the board. This consists of three pieces of cardboard or styrene sheet that are stuck to the board with either adhesive or double-sided sticky tape. The latter is better, as it allows the strips of material to be moved if various widths of glass are to be cut. These three strips are arranged so that glass can be slid onto the board, the three pieces of card holding it firmly in place and preventing movement. The base of the circle cutter is placed on the glass exactly in the middle. This should be determined as the jig is being made and a line marked so that the circle cutter scores the glass in exactly the same place every time. As the strip of glass is cut and broken it is an easy matter to cut the convex glass square again using a set square, and repeat the process. Using this method, a perfect male and female semi-circle can be cut in different pieces of glass, ensuring that they fit perfectly together time and again (see Fig. 23).

If a circle cutter is not available, a similar effect can be achieved using French curves or a circular lid and tracing the outline onto the glass. By

Fig. 23 Cutting semi-circles.

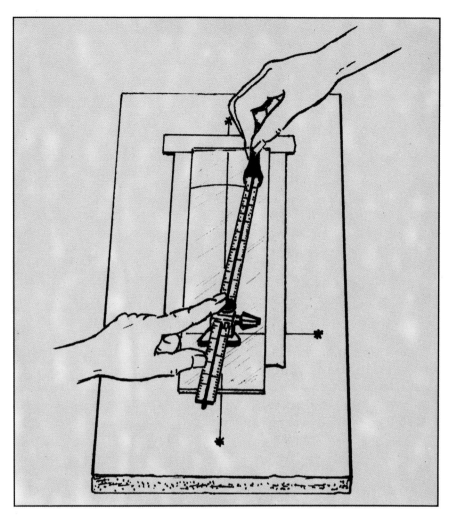

carefully following the outline with a cutter, a similar result can be obtained. Provided that the semi-circle is not too small, the scoreline can either be broken out by hand or using pliers, in fact treated as a normal straight cut.

FOILING THE GLASS

The glass to be foiled should be perfectly clean and free from any dirt or grease. The edges should be free from any irregularities. Before commencing foiling, it is a good idea to place the relevant pieces of glass together to make sure that they are all exactly the same size and shape. The strength and elegance of the finished structure will greatly depend on the neat application of the foil, as this acts as a membrane onto which the final soldering is applied.

Strip the protective backing from a short length of copperfoil tape. Consult p. 36 if in doubt as to which width you should use. Place the glass centrally on the tape so that an even overlap results when the foil is pressed to the sides of the glass. Work the foil around the glass, stripping the protective backing away as necessary. Foil all of the edges of the glass

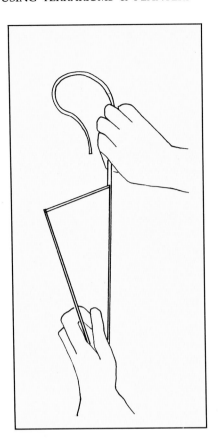

Fig. 24 Foiling the glass.

and allow a 6 mm to 8 mm overlap (see Fig. 24). If foiling concave glass, foil the curved part first as it is more difficult to get it to stay in place. Crimp the foil, slowly pressing it in place as you go.

Folding the Foil onto the Glass

Fold the foil onto the glass using the fingers. Care should be taken when overlapping the corners, as the foil can be very sharp at these points, and painful, cut fingers can be the result of careless handling. After folding, the foiled glass should be placed on a flat surface and the foil thoroughly burnished onto the surface of the glass, using a hardwood fid or any suitable piece of shaped wood. Try not to be too heavy-handed, when smoothing the foil onto the glass, as it can easily tear if a thin gauge.

If, at this stage, the foiling is found to be uneven, there are two alternatives. Either cut the uneven side back with a craft knife or strip the foil off and start again. If the foiled glass is not to be assembled straight away, it is a good idea to wrap it in a piece of old newspaper to prevent the foil from oxidising.

Tinning the Foil

The foil should now be coated with solder. This has two advantages: it greatly strengthens the foil, and it makes it easier to tack solder the structure together when the time comes. The foil should at first be coated

Dried Helichrysum, Gypsophila *and Glycerined* Beech (Fagus) *with Bracken* (Pteridium) *were used for this eye-catching display.*

An attractive table centre using Escallonia *(two shades),* Sweet William (Dianthus barbatus) *and* Campanula.

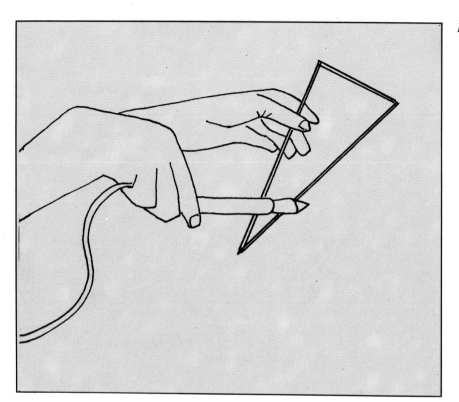

Fig. 25 *Tinning the foil.*

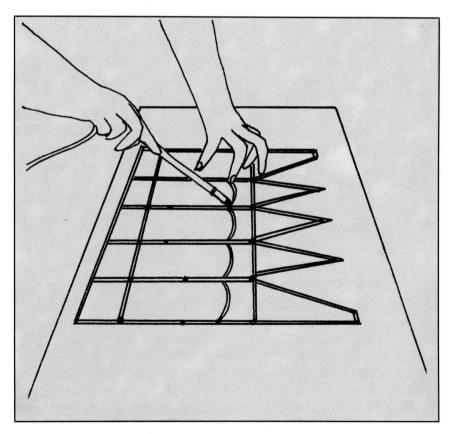

Fig. 26 *Assembling and tack soldering the foiled pieces.*

thinly with flux to remove any oxidisation. If the foiled pieces have been left for any length of time, with the result that they have become heavily oxidised, it is best to polish the foil with a piece of very fine grade wire wool before applying the flux.

After fluxing, take a small blob of solder on the tip of the soldering iron and wipe all of the foiled surfaces with it, renewing the solder as necessary, until all of the foiled surfaces are coated with the solder (see Fig. 25). Wipe any excess flux off the foil after it has been tinned to prevent it staining the glass. Never leave the flux on the foil without applying solder as this will cause problems later on.

Tack Soldering

The object of tack soldering is to make a thin solder joint using just enough solder to join the pieces of foiled glass together. These act as hinges to allow the pieces of glass to be folded and tacked together into the terrarium's final shape. A mere wipe across the joints with a lightly tinned iron is all that is required (see Fig. 26). Re-fluxing the joints should not be necessary, but if difficulty is encountered then it may be found to be an advantage. Avoid making too thick a solder joint as this will result in the copperfoil tearing away from the glass during final assembly. Make at least two tack solder joints on each edge that is to be joined. Where the pieces of glass are joined, but will not be folded (on the base section for instance) the solder joints need not be as critical.

ASSEMBLING THE TERRARIUM

Place the foiled and tinned pieces of glass onto a perfectly flat surface and assemble them as shown. It is now that any mis-cut pieces of glass will become apparent. If any pieces are found to be badly cut or out of square, it is best to replace them at this stage.

Make the tack joints to join each piece of glass to the next. Do this whilst the assembled pieces are still flat on the worktop. Then, starting with either the right or left end panels, carefully lift and fold the assembly towards the middle. At the same time, fold the triangular top pieces together so that the tips meet. Quickly flux the joint at the apex and apply a blob of solder to secure the two pieces together. Fold up the opposite side and secure the apex of the joint in a similar manner.

Care should be taken at this stage as the tack solder joints of the middle pieces that still remain on the workbench will be under some strain, and a poorly-made joint could be liable to fail.

Take the two sides that have been soldered, one side in each hand, and carefully lift the structure and place it on its base. This will relieve the strain on the middle joints. Now, with care, fold the top pieces so that they all meet at the top, and secure with a further two solder joints (see Fig. 27). If, at this stage, it is found that some of the foil has torn away from the glass because of poor tack soldering, simply rub down the affected area and overlap a fresh piece of foil, ensuring to burnish the fresh foil over the damaged section.

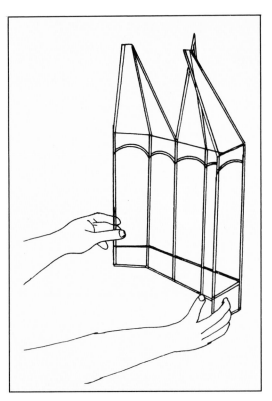

Fig. 27 Bringing the two sides together for soldering.

Fig. 28 Cutting the mirrorback.

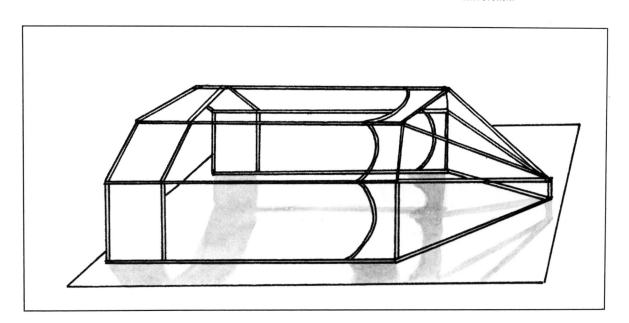

CUTTING THE MIRRORBACK

Place a piece of suitable mirrored glass onto the cutting table. It should be of sufficient size to overlap the assembled structure on all sides. Carefully lift the assembled pieces, remembering that they are very fragile at this stage as they are only held together with flimsy joints. Place them on the

A true miniature greenhouse.

Pressed, dried ivies and glycerined ferns sandwiched between two sheets of glass make an interesting picture. The stained glass frame consists of fractures and streamers (top and bottom) with ordinary green rolled glass for the two sides.

mirror and, holding them down with just enough pressure to prevent movement, trace the outline onto the reflective surface.

Cut the mirror to the traced outline (see Fig. 28). After cutting, it should be foiled and tinned as described earlier. Care should be taken not to let the flux remain on the mirrored back as certain types of flux attack the silvering if left on for too long. When the mirrored back has been cut, foiled and tinned, it should be tack soldered on to the back of the assembled structure. Use about six or eight joints to ensure that the structure is fairly rigid.

FOILING THE INSIDE OF THE GLASS

Before bead soldering is attempted, it is a wise precaution to run a piece of copperfoil tape down the inside of each joint to prevent the molten solder dropping through any gaps that are left between the glass (see Fig. 29). It is best to use as narrow a width of tape as possible, just in case the solder penetrates the adhesive and fuses the two thicknesses of foil together, making it hard to remove after soldering.

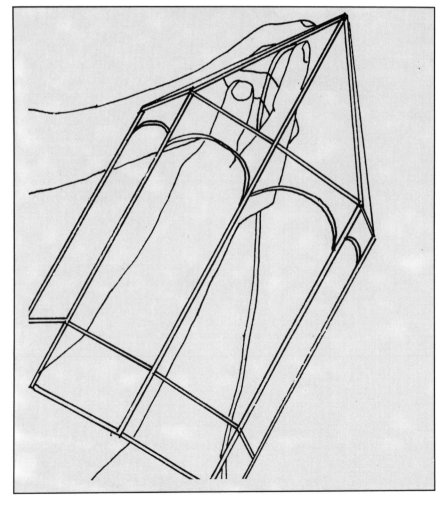

Fig. 29 Foiling the inside of the glass.

Fig. 30 Bead soldering.

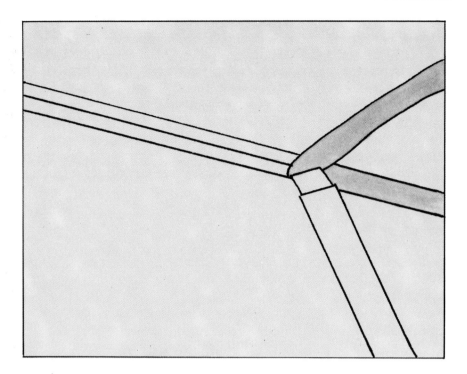

BEAD SOLDERING

The object of bead soldering a three-dimensional object such as a terrarium or planter is to fill the seams that have appeared between the pieces of foiled glass during assembly with solder, and to build this solder up until a neatly rounded bead can be made on top to achieve an attractive finish. Solder, when heated, turns to liquid and in such form flows along the copperfoil tape until it cools and hardens. Molten solder can be a painful medium to work with if it is not treated with respect. Always wear either an apron or an overall to protect clothing, as solder is difficult to remove once it hardens. The joint to be made should always be presented to the soldering iron on a horizontal plane, as this helps the solder to flow evenly along the seam.

Polish the seam to be made with a little piece of wire wool and then thoroughly flux the two halves. Sandwich a stick of solder between the joint and the soldering iron tip. Press the tip down onto the solder which will turn to liquid and flow along the joint. Lift the solder and the iron as soon as the solder melts and move further along the seam; repeat the process until the complete seam has been coated with solder (see Fig. 30). The result may be a little lumpy, but do not be discouraged. Simply re-flux the solder and, starting at the top of the seam and keeping the assembly horizontal, work the soldering iron down the seam, melting the solder until an even, rounded bead of solder is achieved. If any low spots appear, simply add more solder to even them up. Allow the solder a few seconds to cool before moving the assembly.

It is best to solder down the longest seams first, starting at the top and working down. This helps to strengthen the structure. Where two joints meet or overlap, it is sometimes necessary to re-flux and re-work the joint. Remember to keep the seam being made on a perfectly horizontal plane, as this will help the molten solder flow in an even bead. After all the joints have been soldered to your satisfaction, carefully peel off the copperfoil tape from inside the glass. If any solder has managed to penetrate the tape and has formed blobs of solder inside, take the soldering iron tip and smooth them out.

BASE CUTTING

After bead soldering has been completed, place the structure on a suitable piece of glass and, as with the mirrorback, trace the design for the base onto it. It is best to make a note of which way round the base will fit. Mark the left and right edges on the glass. Cut the base, foil it and tack and bead solder it to the bottom of the terrarium.

FINISHING THE ASSEMBLY

A piece of copper wire should be obtained at this stage of assembly and fashioned as illustrated in Plates 27 and 28, and Fig. 46. Any solid copper wire is suitable. A good source for this is to strip the plastic insulation from ordinary cable of the type used for domestic house wiring. It is very cheap to buy and a small length will last a long time.

After bending the wire to shape, flux and tin it and solder it into the top of the terrarium. Make sure that the loop is firmly embedded in the solder on either side of the apex as this will have to carry a considerable weight when the finished structure is planted and hung on the wall.

If a door is to be fitted to the terrarium, there are many ways of tackling this. The easiest and most straightforward is to obtain some thin brass channel from the local hobby shop that is just wide enough to take the thickness of the glass. With a junior hacksaw, cut the brass channel to the correct size to fit the opening. The finished result can be much improved if mitred joints are used for each corner of the channel. Polish the brass with wire wool to ensure a good solder joint. Apply flux to the metal and the foil around the opening and carefully solder the channel in place.

The door is then cut to size and slid into place. It is best to rub down the edges of the door with a silicon carbide stone to remove any sharp edges from the glass. Black bronzing salts can be used on the brass to darken it and blend it with the patina of the terrarium. If these are not used, it is best to polish the channel with a file to remove the patina where the solder joints are made. The advantage of using this method for door construction is that the foil around the opening does not have to be strengthened. The only disadvantage is that the door cannot be left partly open to allow for ventilation.

Small brass hinges can be bought ready-made. A good place to look for these are woodwork suppliers or model boat shops. Some are a little large for terrariums, but can sometimes be cut to size using a small pair of tin shears. Care should be taken when soldering them as one blob of solder in the wrong place will result in the hinge becoming a solid mass. To

Petal Planter with Maidenhair Fern (Adiantum), *Polka Dot Plant* (Hypoestus) *and variegated Ivy* (Hedera).

prevent this, apply a drop of oil to the moving part of the hinge to prevent solder entering.

By far the easiest way of making hinges is by using brass or copper tubing of different diameters that simply 'telescope' inside each other. For really small, neat hinges, it is best to use a piece of tubing and some rigid brass or copper wire. Solder the tubing in the middle of the door, making sure it is firmly soldered squarely along the middle of the glass. Cut two more pieces of tubing at either end of the door and pass the smaller diameter wire through all three pieces. Solder this to the two outside pieces to form the hinge. Carefully flux and solder the completed door assembly into the opening. Latches for holding the door closed can be constructed in a similar way. Simply bend a loop in the middle of the wire, then attach it to the door surround, placing another piece of tubing on the opening for it to fit into.

To keep solder away from the moving parts of the hinges and latches, lightly oil the wire. Fitting doors to terrariums needs some degree of patience, and it is best to take into account the thickness of the hinges when cutting the glass for the door. Doors and their surrounds should always be foiled with extra wide foil to take the strains that hinges and latches cause. For 2 mm glass use $7/32$ in (6 mm) or $1/4$ in (6.5 mm) foil. For 3 mm glass use $5/16$ in (8 mm) or $3/8$ in (9.5 mm) foil.

If the terrarium or planter is to stand on a table it should be fitted with either small feet or a piece of non-abrasive material to prevent it scratching the surface. Brass feet can be obtained from specialised suppliers. The feet are simply soldered on. If these are not available, a sheet of cork floor tile is a very useful substitute. Cut into small pieces and stuck to the base, one tile will last for ages. Self-adhesive felt is another material that is useful for covering the base.

Some office supply outlets sell self-adhesive rubber 'bump-ons'. These are little rubber buttons normally used for calculators, typewriters etc. They are also ideal for terrariums and planters.

FINIALS

The dictionary description of a finial is an 'ornament on top of a spire'. This is a very good description of the use of finials for terrarium construction. They are small brass ornaments, either turnings or castings, that are soldered on to the top of terrariums either for decoration or to hide a point where several soldered seams meet.

WASHING FINISHED TERRARIUMS

Wash the finished terrarium in a mixture of warm water and washing-up liquid. It is best to do this as soon as soldering has been completed as certain types of fluxes can mark the glass if they are left on for too long.

Washing also shows if there are any gaps left in between the solder joints. If any are found, simply re-flux the joint and seal the hole with solder. Thoroughly wash all the soldered seams to remove any traces of flux from both inside and outside.

Whilst washing, polish the seams with a small pad of very fine grade wire wool (grade 000 is ideal). If this is not available, then a very mild scouring pad may be used. It is important only to polish the seams with a very mild abrasive as the solder is very soft and any coarse material will score the soft surface, and in due course cause the patina to have a dull finish when it is applied.

It is best not to leave the terrarium immersed in the water for any length of time as this can cause the glue in the foil to solidify and mark the glass. Remove the terrarium from the water and rinse it in clean water a couple of times to disperse any detergent that is left. It is important at this stage to dry the structure completely and polish the glass using a piece of rag or some paper towels. Never leave the terrarium to dry naturally, or detergent smears will dry on the glass. These cause an iridescent stain and should be avoided at all costs as they are very difficult to remove once they have appeared. The terrarium is now ready for the application of whichever patina it has been decided to use, or, of course, the structure can be used as it is with the bright, shiny finish of the solder being left.

PATINA APPLICATION

Bronze Antique Finish

There are nearly as many methods and formulations for applying and mixing the copper sulphate solution that turns solder a copper colour as there are craftsmen using it. Listed below are two suggested methods. Please remember that copper sulphate is *poisonous* and should be kept *well out of the reach of children*. The solution can turn the hands a bright green colour, so *always* wear a pair of rubber gloves and an apron.

Fig. 31 Applying the patina with an old toothbrush.

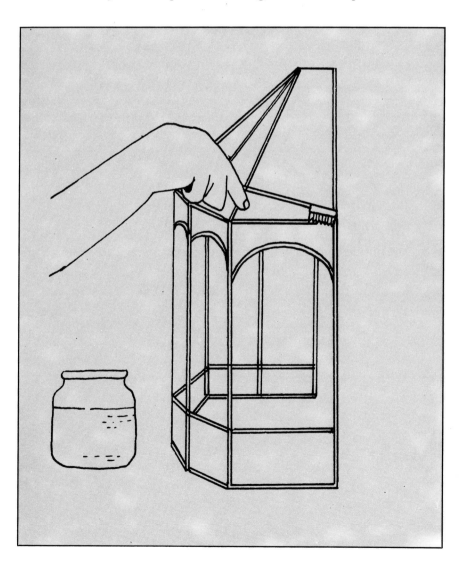

Method 1

Take 500 ml (¾ pint) of hot water and add 100 g (3½ oz) of copper sulphate crystals. Stir them thoroughly until they dissolve. If they do not dissolve, this indicates that the water is not hot enough. Using an old toothbrush or similar, brush the solution, while it is still hot, up and down the soldered seams until a uniform copper patina has been achieved (see Fig. 31).

If the first application is a little patchy, go over the area affected once again. If the patina still will not take, polish the area with a piece of wire wool wetted in the patina solution, and try again. Leave the solution on the solder for about five minutes. Wash the terrarium in a solution of warm water and washing-up liquid, rinse and dry as before. Polish the finished terrarium with a household glass cleaner or a mixture of methylated spirits and water diluted in equal parts.

Buff the glass both inside and out. Final polishing is best carried out in a good light as any marks or stains on the glass are then easy to spot and far easier to remove than when the terrarium is planted. For a really bright, shiny finish, the copper patina can be polished with metal polish. Care should be taken when applying and removing the polish, as vigorous rubbing can remove the patina, leaving the solder showing through. The metal polish is also a good glass cleaner.

Method 2

Dissolve 50 g (1¾ oz) of copper sulphate crystals into 250 ml (9 fl.oz) of hot water as in the previous method, and add to this two or three drops of hydrochloric acid. *Always* add the acid to the solution, *not* the solution to the acid. This solution can be applied either hot or cold. Re-application of the mixture produces a darker and darker finish.

Leave the solution on for at least five minutes, making sure that the patina is an even shade all over. Wash the terrarium in clean, warm water, and thoroughly dry it to prevent any marks on the glass. Polish the patina with a soft cloth or paper towel. The result should be a rich antique copper colour, with a semi-matt finish. Finally, polish all of the glass with household window cleaner or a mixture of methylated spirits and water.

Black Patina

This solution is normally supplied in ready-to-use form. It is a mixture containing selenium dioxide and nitric acid. Therefore, it should be *handled with extreme care. Always* wear rubber gloves and an apron at all times. It is also a good idea to check the gloves for leaks every time you put them on when applying this solution. Needless to say, it should be *kept well out of the reach of children*.

Despite its drawbacks, the finish achieved using this patina is a very attractive dark grey, almost black, colour. It gives the finished terrarium the look of antique lead. Application is similar to that for copper sulphate. After washing and polishing the terrarium, the black patina is brushed up and down the soldered seams, until a uniform dark grey finish has been

This Parasol has a black patina top. The base section is simply polished solder left unstained.

This Diamond Planter has opalescent glass used in the base section to help obscure the root structure of the plants.

achieved. Try to avoid splashes when brushing the solution on. If the solution should go on the skin wash it off using plenty of water. Thoroughly rinse the solution off with clean water, and do this two or three times. Dry the structure as before with a cloth or paper towels. Finally, polish the patina with a soft cloth. Do not use metal polish as this will remove the finish and the solder will show through.

COATING WITH LACQUER

After the terrarium has been finished it may be an advantage to paint it with a coat of clear lacquer. This is a cellulose-based product which, when applied, prevents the patina from oxidising and becoming dull. This is especially useful if the patina has been polished.

The lacquer is easy to obtain from art shops. It is normally used for finishing beaten copper work. The lacquer is best applied with a soft sable or camel-hair brush. Simply paint all the bead soldered seams with it, ensuring that the brush is well loaded with lacquer as it dries very quickly. After the first coat has dried, which is virtually instantly, it is a good idea to apply a second coat to build up the lacquer and ensure even coverage. Two coats help to preserve the shiny finish for a long time. If any lacquer is painted onto the glass, wait until it dries and scrape it off with a knife or razor blade.

ETCHING, SAND BLASTING AND ENGRAVING

Many interesting effects can be produced on glass using simple etching and engraving techniques. When etched or engraved glass panels are incorporated into a terrarium or planter, some really attractive objects can be made. Not only is the finished product different but it can also be more saleable, if the pastime is to be turned into a profitable hobby. People are always looking for something different, so using etched and engraved glass can offer the scope for personalised gifts for weddings, birthdays, anniversaries etc.

ETCHING GLASS

Etching of glass began in the late seventeenth century, but the technique was not really exploited until the invention of hydrofluoric acid in the nineteenth century. It became very popular at about the turn of the twentieth century and some very fine examples of etched glass can still be seen today. Etching glass is basically a technique for removing a fine layer of glass using a hydrofluoric acid solution. When the acid is washed off, a frosting effect is left on the glass.

A 'resist' is applied to the glass before it is etched. A resist is basically a material that prevents the acid reacting with the glass. In the early days of etching the resist was often a wax rosin mixture that had to be melted together and applied to the glass in a liquid state. This was a skill in itself. Today's materials are much easier to use. Most of the materials used for etching can be obtained reasonably easily and many are household items (see Fig. 32). The only two items that a specialist supplier may have to be

Fig. 32 Tools and materials used in etching: 1) pattern sheet, 2) carbon transfer paper, 3) acrylic resist paper, 4) screen etch solution, 5) cellulose sponge, 6) rubber gloves, 7) paint brush, 8) craft knife.

used for is the screen etch solution and the acrylic resist contact sheeting. The screen etch solution is a ready to use, dilute mixture of hydrofluoric acid and aggregate. In this form it has a thick creamy consistency to help the mixture stay in place.

Acrylic resist contact paper is fairly thick plasticised sheeting with a self-adhesive backing. Being acrylic it is easy to cut to shape with a craft knife or scalpel. Other resists can be used, and the most common one

Fig. 33 Patterns for use in etching.

found in most homes is clear nail varnish. If nail varnish is used, ensure that it is thoroughly dry before applying the etch solution. Other acid-resistant tusches may be obtained from art shops.

Patterns for etching can be found in many places. In Fig. 33 a few basic shapes are illustrated, but many more can be found in magazines and newspapers. A good source is children's colouring books.

To make an etched design on glass proceed as follows. Take a piece of resist sheet and cut it to the same size of the glass that is to be etched. Thoroughly clean the glass of dirt and grease with either methylated spirits or a household glass cleaner. Carefully peel back a small portion of

Parasol planted with Parlour Palm (Chamaedora) *and a number of different* Fittonia *and a* Pilea.

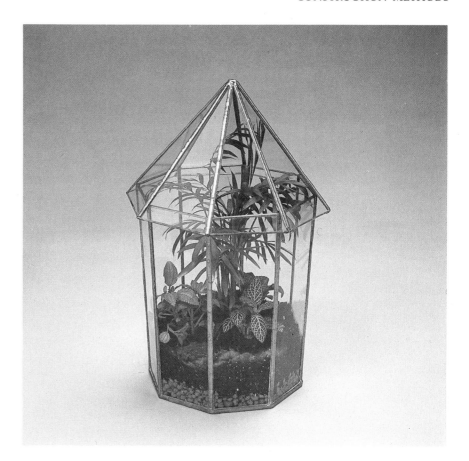

Carousel. The coloured glass used in the roof section is inexpensive Cathedral glass.

the backing paper and stick the resist onto the glass. It is best to start at one corner. With a piece of rag or paper towel, smooth the sheet out across the glass, stripping the backing off at the same time. Make sure to smooth out any bubbles or creases that become trapped between the glass and the sheet of resist. If any do appear, lift the sheet up and smooth it down again.

If an illustration from this book is to be used, it is best to make a copy of it on to a sheet of plain paper to save ruining the page. To do this proceed as when making a template. Place a sheet of carbon paper (carbonised side down) over a piece of plain paper and trace the design through from the printed illustration. Remember to place a sheet of tracing paper over the page to prevent it being ruined. Trace the design completely, starting with the outline and then shading in the middle.

Transfer the finished design on to the resist using a similar method. Place the carbon paper down onto the resist and then trace the design through it. As with making the templates, ensure that the design does not move as it is being transferred. Before removing the design, gently lift a corner to ensure that the pattern is on the resist paper. With a scalpel or craft knife, carefully cut round the outline of the transferred design. Make sure to use a sharp blade when cutting out, as a blunt one can scratch the glass and make cutting the resist an uphill task. Only use sufficient pressure to cut the resist paper.

Starting at one corner, lift the resist with the point of the knife and carefully peel it away. Clean the glass again prior to etching. Use a dabbing motion to prevent damaging the design. The etching solution is perfectly safe if used with respect, so *always* wear rubber gloves and avoid splashing it. It is also advisable to open a window to allow for ventilation.

Prior to applying, stir the mixture with a wooden spatula to ensure that it is thoroughly mixed. Apply the etching cream with a small paint brush, brushing the mixture on gently in one direction only. Be generous when applying it, building up a layer of about 3 mm (⅛ in) thick, and make sure that the cream is worked into all of the corners. Leave the mixture to react with the glass. The time is usually stated on the container, but it would normally be about five minutes. After this, wash the glass under running water until all traces of the cream have been removed. Dry the glass with a piece of rag or paper towel and then peel off the sheet of resist.

Finally, polish the etched glass and examine the end result. The glass can now be foiled in the normal way and incorporated into the terrarium or planter.

There are several companies who supply rub-on transfers that have been designed specifically for the etched glass hobbyist. There are many designs available. The great advantage of using these is that they are quicker to use than resist paper and the designs tend to be more intricate. However, care should be taken when using them. A delicate touch is needed when rubbing the design onto the glass as the backing paper tends to 'cockle' on large designs and also the transfer is very thin so vigorous brushing with the etching cream can cause problems. If used correctly, however, these rub-on designs produce some very pleasing effects. If these transfers are not readily available, a similar effect can be obtained using the rub-on instant lettering sold by many stationers and graphic art shops.

SAND BLASTING

The sand blasting of glass dates back only about one hundred years. At first the glass was blasted with iron particles, but today different grades of sand are used. The technique is very similar to etching glass, in many ways. The resist is prepared in a similar fashion, using the same materials, after which the glass is simply blasted with sand. The end result, although comparable to etching, has a deeper abraded texture, depending on which grit size of sand has been used and the length of time for which the glass is blasted.

Sand blasting is normally outside the scope of the amateur, as an expensive spray gun and compressor have to be used. It is, however, well worth trying to find a company locally with the equipment that would be willing to carry out the work. Many are quite willing to sand blast small amounts of glass.

GLASS ENGRAVING

The art of engraving on glass dates back to the sixteenth century. It was the Venetians who initially used diamond-impregnated etching tools for glass engraving. It quickly spread to Germany, Holland, Bohemia and England. Indeed, the Venetian, Giacomo Vercellini, established a virtual monopoly in England and his engraved glasses were the exclusive privilege of Queen Elizabeth 1. The seventeenth century saw a notable increase in this skill in Holland and many amateur exponents of the art acquired a reputation for their work.

There are many ways of engraving glass, most of them requiring some sort of mechanical device. These are either diamond-tipped tools that are used with a grinding machine fitted with a flexible shaft, or small hand-held engraving machines that use an oscillating motion to remove the glass from the surface. There are also of course the more expensive engraving/brilliant cutting machines, that are normally too expensive for the amateur glassworker to contemplate. There is, however, a method of hand engraving that has become popular in recent years and is relatively inexpensive.

It was originally developed in Switzerland in the early 1970s, and glass engraving has now become a very popular hobby amongst the Swiss. The technique is fairly simple and easy to learn. Another advantage is that, if in due course an engraving machine is bought, similar techniques can be adopted. The tools that are available (see Fig. 34) have tiny particles of industrial diamond impregnated into various sizes of needle.

They can be bought individually or more normally in a kit containing pattern sheets, the diamond etching tools and a piece of black felt to place the glass on. Some designs are shown in Fig. 35, but many other patterns

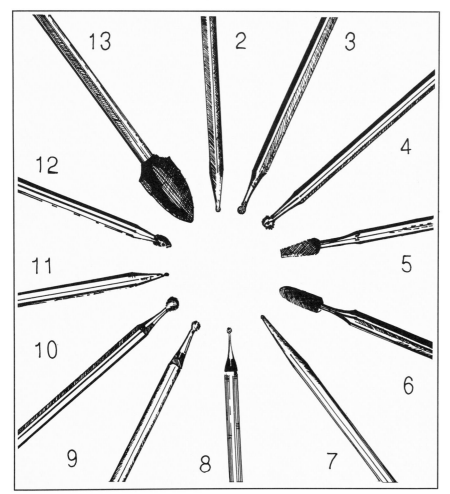

Fig. 34 Tools used in hand glass engraving: 2–4) standard ballpoint; 5–6) small and large carborundum tips; 7) diamond point; 8–10) special ballpoint needles (diamond dust); 11) miniature ballpoint for very fine work; 12) diamond flame-diamond dust needle; 13) glass rubber to slightly roughen glass.

are available or, of course, your own design can be used. Any thickness or type of glass can be used, although it is better to use 2 mm or possibly 3 mm plain glass, as it is easier to follow the outline of the pattern. Thicker glass tends to refract the pattern, making it harder to follow.

The basic technique is similar to sketching with a pencil, except that instead of being grey the transparent glass surface becomes white and opaque. By gradually wearing the glass away, definite contours in the glass are achieved. It is best to practise on a piece of scrap glass before any patterns are attempted (see Fig. 36).

First draw a series of squares about 13 mm (½ in) square, with a fine needle, using just enough pressure to score the glass. Using a medium needle and exerting a small amount of pressure, lightly scratch the surface using vertical parallel lines to take the shiny surface from the glass. It is best to get the feel of the tool, trying to stay within the guide lines that were first drawn. Go over the vertical lines in the same direction, gradually building up the pressure with the needle until the complete square has a uniform finish. If any corners have been missed, go over them using the fine grounding needle. It is best to work slowly,

Fig. 35 (Opposite) Patterns for hand glass engraving.

Fig. 36 Examples of right and wrong strokes.

'building up' the engraving as work progresses. It should always be remembered that work can always be added to but once a line is engraved it cannot be erased. If a line is engraved in the wrong place, a white chinagraph pencil with a fine point can be used to draw on the glass to see if the intended correction will look all right.

Always keep the working area free from glass dust by wiping it away with a piece of rag or paper towel. *Never* blow the glass dust away. Select a pattern that is not too difficult to start with. A simple flower pattern is ideal. Place the piece of glass over the pattern and trace the outline using the fine needle with just enough pressure to mark the glass. Once the outline has been drawn, the pattern can be removed. It is best to place the glass on a dark, preferably black, surface. The shading and finishing can then be built up as indicated by the pattern.

Further Techniques
Glass Drawing (Fig. 37)

This is a technique where simple horizontal and vertical lines are engraving so that shaded surfaces are indicated by parallel lines.

Stippling (Fig. 38)

This is a simple method where the tip of the needle is lightly tapped on the surface of the glass. This can be employed for light, delicate effects such as blossoms or flower heads.

Fling Strokes (Fig. 39)

As the name implies, the tip of the needle (normally a fine needle) is moved across the glass in light flinging movements. These sort of strokes are well suited for drawing animal fur, whiskers, and the small hairs on flowers and petals etc.

Fig. 37 Glass drawing.

Fig. 38 Stippling.

Fig. 39 Fling strokes.

The hand glass engraving technique is a method well worth experimenting with not only for terrariums but also for engraving other glass objects such as wine glasses, decanters and vases. If this method of glass engraving is to be used, a few important points should be remembered at all times. *Never* blow away the glass dust, but *always* wipe with a rag or paper towel. Try to use engraving strokes one way. Cross-hatching will not only look ineffective but it will also damage the engraving needles in a similar manner to overscoring glass with a glass-cutter.

Black Diamond Planter. Dried flowers used are Statice, Quaking Grass (Briza), Honesty (Lunaria) *and* Larkspur (Delphinium).

Some of the many attractive houseplants suitable for terrariums.

5 Terrariums and Planters to Make

PETAL PLANTER (FIG. 40)

Mirror Glass – 305 mm × 195 mm (12 × 8 in)
Clear Glass – 580 cm² (90 sq. in)
Solder – 0.25 kg (½ lb)
Copperfoil – ¼ roll (8.2 m or 9 yd)

A simple mirrorback planter with semi-circular back. This design can be modified if a circle cutter is not available. Square pieces of glass arranged in a graduated pattern can still look attractive. The mirror can be cut to a point, and the petals shown can be omitted if no coloured glass can be obtained.

Method of Construction

1. Make an accurate set of templates.
2. Mark and cut the glass.
3. Foil the pieces of glass.
4. Apply flux and tin each piece in turn.
5. Cut the mirror to the dimensions shown in the diagram.
6. Cut the mirror. It is a wise precaution when cutting the semi-circle to make some secondary scorelines (see 'Victorian', p. 79). Tap the mirror on the underside of the scoreline to make it run.
7. Foil and tin the mirror.
8. Lay the seven pieces of foiled glass on the work surface. Arrange them as shown in the diagram. Tack solder them together.
9. Lift either end and stand the assembled pieces upright.
10. Prop the mirror against a book or a cardboard box and tack solder either end of the foiled pieces to either side of the mirror.
11. Place the assembly on the piece of glass that is to form the base.
12. Carefully arrange the pieces of glass to the angles shown on the base section of the diagram. The two outer sides should be at right angles to the mirrorback and the front parallel to it. The other four pieces should be at the angles shown.
13. Gently hold the pieces down and trace the outline onto the glass underneath.
14. Lift the assembly off the base.
15. Cut, foil and tin the base section.
16. Tack solder the assembly onto the base.

Fig. 40 Petal Planter.

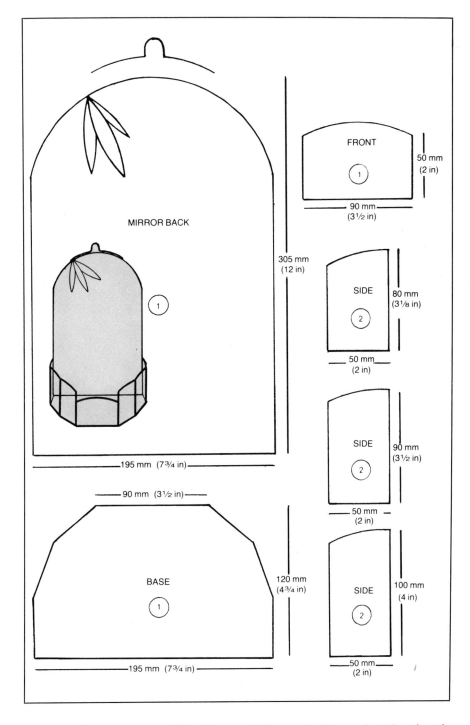

17. Apply a narrow width of copperfoil tape to the underside of each joint. Remove the tape after bead soldering.
18. Bead solder the assembly and also the foiled edge of the mirror.
19. Fashion a piece of copper wire to the shape shown in the diagram and solder it in place.
20. Wash, polish and stain with whichever patina is preferred.

DIAMOND PLANTER (FIG. 41)

Glass – 1500 cm² (1.6 sq. ft)
Solder – 0.5 kg (1 lb)
Copperfoil – ¼ roll (8.2 m or 9 yd)

This simple little planter can be assembled using either small or large triangular pieces of glass. One word of caution, however: make sure that the hanging loop is securely soldered into place.

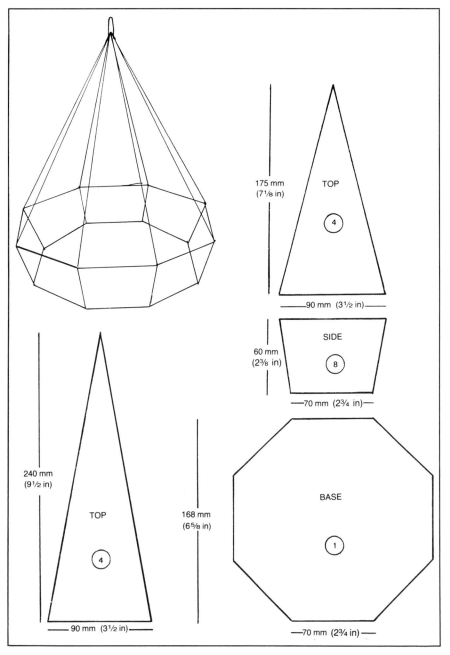

175 mm
(7⅛ in)

TOP

4

90 mm (3½ in)

SIDE

8

60 mm
(2⅜ in)

70 mm (2¾ in)

240 mm
(9½ in)

TOP

4

168 mm
(6⅝ in)

BASE

1

90 mm (3½ in)

70 mm (2¾ in)

Fig. 41 Diamond Planter.

Method of Construction

1. Make an accurate set of templates.
2. Mark and cut the glass.
3. Foil the pieces of glass.
4. Apply flux and tin each piece in turn.
5. Arrange the side sections on the worktop. They should form a wide semi-circle. Tack solder them together.
6. Gently lift the two outer pieces and fold the assembly until the pieces meet. The other pieces should all remain flat on the worktop. Tack solder the joints where the two sides meet.
7. Lift the assembled pieces onto the piece of glass that will form the base.
8. Whilst gently pressing down, mark the outline of the base on the glass.
9. Remove the assembled pieces.
10. Cut, foil and tin the base section.
11. Tack solder the assembly onto the base.
12. Tack solder the four triangular pieces to the base section. Assemble them two at a time. Ensure that they are firmly joined at the top.
13. Apply a narrow width of copperfoil tape to the underside of each joint. Remove tape after bead soldering.
14. Proceed to bead solder the complete assembly.
15. Fashion a small hanging hook from copper wire. Flux and solder the wire at the tip of the four triangular pieces. Be generous with the solder when securing the hook.
16. Wash, polish and stain with whichever patina is preferred.

THE VICTORIAN (FIG. 42)

Glass – 8850 cm² (9½ sq. ft)
Solder – 1 kg (2.2 lb)
Copperfoil – 1 roll (33 m or 36 yd)

The Victorian, although a large and impressive-looking structure, is in fact very easy to build and well within the scope of the beginner. If being built as a first project and the use of so much glass and solder seems a little extravagant, the model could be scaled down. For a half-scale model simply halve all of the dimensions given.

Either 2 mm or 3 mm glass can be used although the corner solder joints will be less noticeable if 2 mm glass is employed. Many of the glass panels are simply squares of glass and so no actual templates are shown, only the dimensions. The top sections C and D are the same shape although obviously C is longer than D.

Method of Construction

1. Make an accurate set of templates.
2. Mark and cut the glass. If a circle cutter is not available it is quite

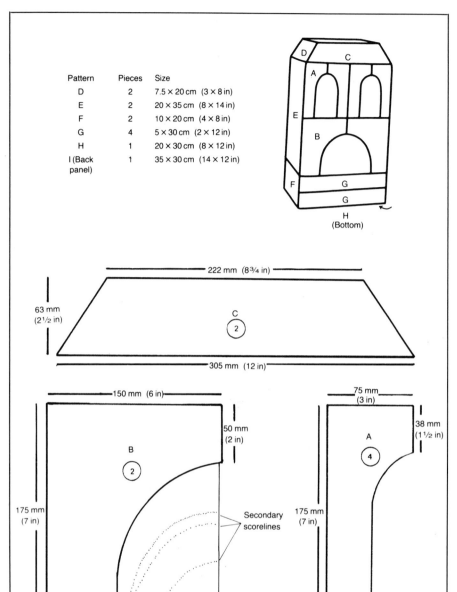

Fig. 42 The Victorian.

Pattern	Pieces	Size
D	2	7.5 × 20 cm (3 × 8 in)
E	2	20 × 35 cm (8 × 14 in)
F	2	10 × 20 cm (4 × 8 in)
G	4	5 × 30 cm (2 × 12 in)
H	1	20 × 30 cm (8 × 12 in)
I (Back panel)	1	35 × 30 cm (14 × 12 in)

permissible to cut the corners freehand. Before breaking out the curve, make a number of secondary scorelines as shown on B. Tap and break each scoreline in turn, working inwards toward the actual scoreline. If there are any uneven edges nibble them away using a pair of grozing pliers.

3. Foil the pieces of glass, trying to ensure an even overlap.
4. Apply flux and tin each piece in turn.
5. Assemble each of the four sides in turn. Tack solder the relevant

pieces of glass together, ensuring that all of the pieces fit together neatly. Ensure that the work surface is flat.

6. Carefully lift and turn the panels over and commence bead soldering. Taping the underside of each panel to prevent molten solder dropping through the joints should not be necessary as they are being soldered on a flat surface.

    Do not bead solder the joint between sections C and D and the main assembly as it will need to be folded during final assembly.

7. After all of the four panels have been assembled and bead soldered, take a front and a side panel and place them square to each other, and where the two panels meet flux and tack solder them together. Fold sections C and D together and flux and tack solder these together.

    Repeat this with the other two sections. Join the four sections together to form a tall, oblong box. Check with a set square that the structure is square.

8. Carefully lift the assembly onto the piece of glass that will form the base.

9. Mark the outline of the structure on the sheet of glass.

10. Remove the structure, then cut, foil and tin the base.

11. Lift the structure back onto the base and apply a few generous blobs of solder to join them together. It should now be reasonably rigid.

12. Bead solder the base and the four corner joints.

13. Wash, polish and stain with whichever patina is preferred.

GAZEBO (FIG. 43)

Glass – 5048 cm^2 (5½ sq. ft)
Solder – 1 kg (2.2 lb)
Copperfoil – 1 roll (33 m or 36 yd)

The Gazebo, although not an ideal first project, is not as difficult as it looks. It is really two mirrorbacks (described in Chapter 4) back to back, with a few pieces of glass added to the middle section to stretch it. If a circle cutter is not available the small semi-circular pieces of glass shown can either be omitted, or oblong pieces can be used instead.

Method of Construction

1. Make accurate templates.
2. Mark and cut the glass.
3. Foil the glass ensuring an even overlap.
4. Apply flux and tin each piece of glass.
5. The two end sections are the same as the mirrorback. They should be assembled as described in Chapter 4. Only proceed to the stage where they are tacked and folded together to allow them to stand on their own.
6. Take two base sections A and two of the large side sections B and

Rocket—a suitable terrarium for single tall subjects.

(Opposite) A Diamond Planter makes an attractive table centre. This one is planted with spray Chrysanthemums, Philadelphus, *variegated* Mint (Mentha), *Marjoram* (Origanum), *Golden Privet* (Ligustrum) *and Golden Cypresses* (Taxodium).

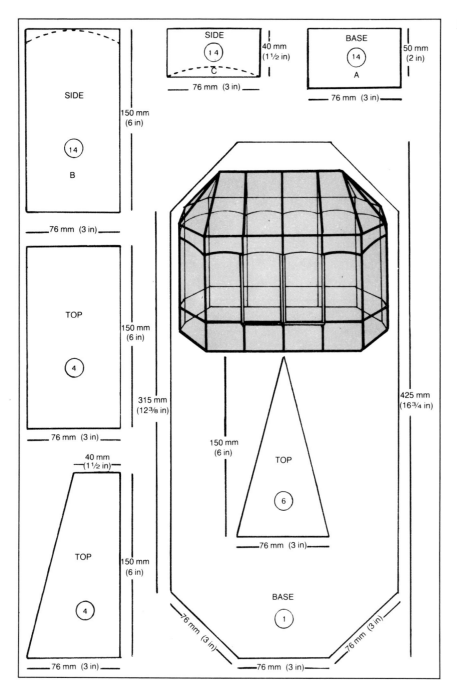

Fig. 43 Gazebo.

assemble them on a flat surface. Add the two pieces of oblong or semi-circular glass C, and assemble them to form a square. Tack solder together. This will form one side section.

7. Place the two previously assembled end sections onto the piece of glass that will form the base. They should be placed back to back and about 15 cm (6 in) apart.

8. Tack solder the side sections to each end of the end sections.

9. Tack solder two more base sections A to form a long oblong. (This

will be the base section for the opposite side.)

10. Tack solder two of the small side sections C together. (This forms the opening above the door.)
11. Tack solder both top and base sections into place.
12. Proceed with the roof sections in a similar manner. Tack solder the four roof panels in place.
13. Draw the outline of the base onto the glass.
14. Carefully lift the assembly off the base.
15. Cut, foil and tin the base section.
16. Tack solder the assembly onto the base.
17. Place a narrow width of copperfoil tape behind each joint. Remove the tape after bead soldering.
18. Bead solder the structure.
19. Obtain some brass channel slightly wider than the glass and manufacture a door surround from it.
20. Wash, polish and stain with whichever patina is preferred.

PARASOL (FIG. 44)

Glass – 2300 cm^2 (2.5 sq. ft)
Solder – 0.75 kg (1½ lb)
Copperfoil – ½ roll (16.5 m or 18 yd)

The Parasol is best constructed in two separate pieces, the top being made before the base section. An attractive finish is to leave the base section in bright shiny solder and stain the top with black patina.

Method of Construction

1. Make an accurate set of templates.
2. Mark and cut the glass.
3. Foil the glass ensuring an even overlap.
4. Apply flux and tin each piece of glass.
5. Assemble the eight triangular pieces that form the top. Place them side by side. They should form a semi-circle. Tack solder them together.
6. Gently lift each end in turn and fold the pieces together to form a cone shape. Join the end pieces with a few generous blobs of solder.
7. The assembly is very weak and flimsy at this stage. While the pieces are on the flat surface, flux each joint in turn and run a generous amount of solder between the joints to make the structure more rigid. Appearance is not important at this stage.
8. Take the eight pieces of glass that form the base section, assemble and tack solder them in a similar manner to the top. As with the top, lift the two outside pieces and gently fold the structure until the two end pieces can be tack soldered together.
9. Lift the assembly onto the piece of glass that is to form the base.

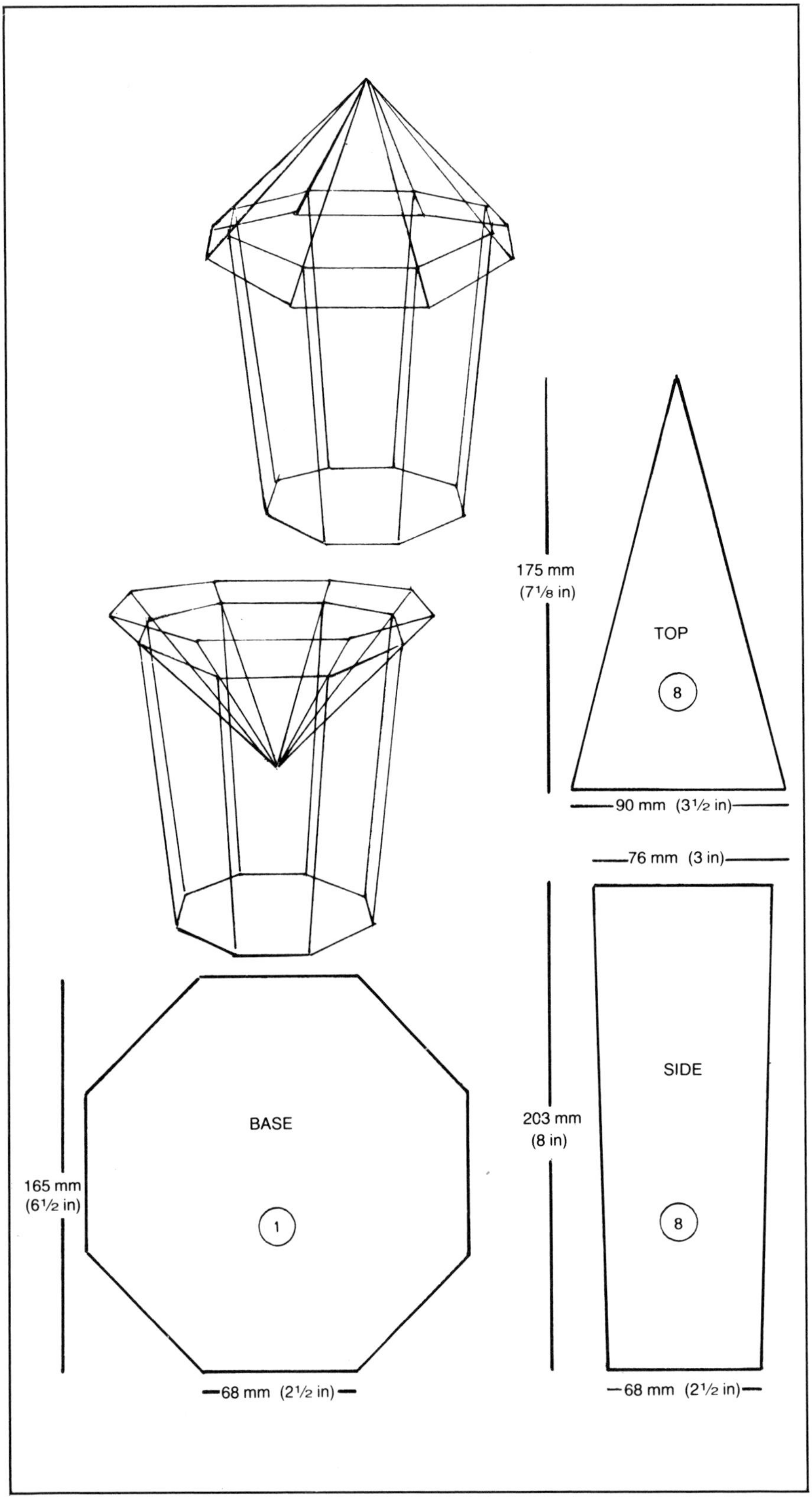

Fig. 44 Parasol.

175 mm
(7⅛ in)

TOP

⑧

— 90 mm (3½ in) —

—76 mm (3 in)—

203 mm
(8 in)

SIDE

⑧

BASE

①

165 mm
(6½ in)

—68 mm (2½ in)—

—68 mm (2½ in)—

The black patina finish helps show off the etched glass panels to good effect.

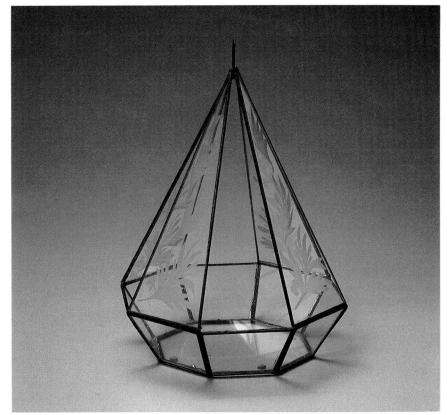

Gazebo, Tiniarium, Mirrorback, Diamond Planter.

Carefully arrange the pieces of glass in a way that each is at roughly the same angle as the next.

10. Invert the top into the base section (see diagram). This will help to ensure that all of the foiled pieces are at the same angle to each other.

11. Draw the outline of the base onto the glass.

12. Remove the assembled pieces from the base.

13. Cut, foil and tin the base section.

14. Place the assembly back onto the base. If it does not fit turn it around until it does.

15. Tack solder the base to the base section.

16. Apply a narrow width of copperfoil tape to the underside of each joint to both top and base sections. Remove the tape after bead soldering.

17. Handling both structures with care, apply the bead soldering.

18. Wash, polish and stain with whichever patina is preferred.

ROCKET (FIG. 45)

Glass – 2600 cm^2 (2.8 sq. ft)
Solder – 0.5 kg (1 lb)
Copperfoil – ¼ roll (8.2 m or 9 yd)

The Rocket is a small, six-sided terrarium which is very suitable for displaying tall plants such as the Parlour Palm (*Chamaedorea elegans*) or the Asparagus Fern (*Asparagus plumosa*). Note should be taken of the hinge and latch assembly. They are made from a piece of brass wire telescoped inside a length of brass tubing.

Method of Construction

1. Make an accurate set of templates.

2. Mark and cut the glass.

3. Foil the pieces of glass ensuring an even overlap. The pieces that form the door and surround must be foiled with wider tape.

4. Apply flux and tin each piece of glass.

5. Lay the six side pieces that join the base on a flat surface. Assemble them side by side so that they form a large semi-circle. Tack solder each piece to its neighbour.

6. Gently lift each end and fold them until they meet. Ensure that all pieces are touching the flat surface. Tack solder the two end pieces together.

7. Lift the assembled pieces onto the piece of glass that will form the base.

8. Whilst pressing gently down, trace the outline onto the base. Mark the base and the assembled glass so that they can be put together again. A cross on two relevant sides will suffice.

9. Cut, foil and tin the base.

Fig. 45 Rocket.

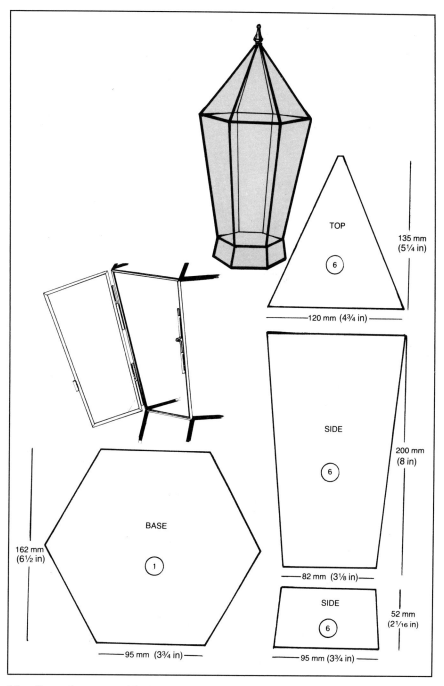

TOP
⑥
135 mm (5¼ in)
120 mm (4¾ in)

SIDE
⑥
200 mm (8 in)
82 mm (3⅛ in)

SIDE
⑥
52 mm (2¹⁄₁₆ in)
95 mm (3¾ in)

BASE
①
162 mm (6½ in)
95 mm (3¾ in)

10. Lay the assembled section over the base and tack solder them together.

11. Taking each of the upper side sections in turn, tack solder them to the base section and to the adjoining side section. Only five sections should be joined in this way as the sixth forms the door.

12. Repeat with the top section, folding them into the apex.

13. Apply a few generous blobs of solder along the joints to make the structure rigid.

14. Apply a narrow width of copperfoil tape to the underside of each joint. Remove the tape after bead soldering.
15. Handling the structure with care, apply the bead soldering.
16. Solder the two hinges to the door and attach it to the door surround.
17. Wash, polish and stain with whichever patina is preferred.

TINIARIUM (FIG. 46)

Glass – 4600 cm^2 (5 sq. ft)
Solder – 0.25 kg (½ lb)
Copperfoil – ¼ roll (8.2 m or 9 yd)

The Tiniarium is a very small structure. The dimensions can of course be altered if necessary to increase its size. Being small, it makes an ideal sample piece. It looks particularly attractive if made in 2 mm glass.

Method of Construction

1. Make an accurate set of templates.
2. Mark and cut the glass.
3. Foil the pieces of glass.
4. Apply flux and tin each piece of glass.
5. The Tiniarium can be constructed in two ways. Either cut the base section first and then tack solder sections A and B to it, and continue to build up the structure by tack soldering sections C and D on top of them, finishing off by soldering the top pieces, E and F, into place. The alternative is to assemble all of the foiled pieces of glass on the worktop and tack solder together in the more conventional manner, folding and tack soldering the structure into shape shown in the diagram.
6. After the structure has been tacked together, place it on the piece of glass that will form the base (ignore this if the first method of construction is being used). Gently pressing down, mark the outline of the base onto the glass.
7. Remove the structure from the glass.
8. Cut, foil and tin the base section.
9. Tack solder the assembly onto the base.
10. Apply a narrow width of copperfoil tape to the underside of each joint. This may be a little fiddly due to the narrow door opening. Remove the tape after bead soldering.
11. Bead solder the assembly.
12. Mark, cut, foil and solder the top of the structure in the same manner used for making the base section.
13. Using brass channel, cut to the appropriate length, solder at the top and bottom of the door opening to form runners for the door to slot into. (See diagram.)
14. Wash, polish and stain with whichever patina is preferred.

Fig. 46 (Opposite) Tiniarium.

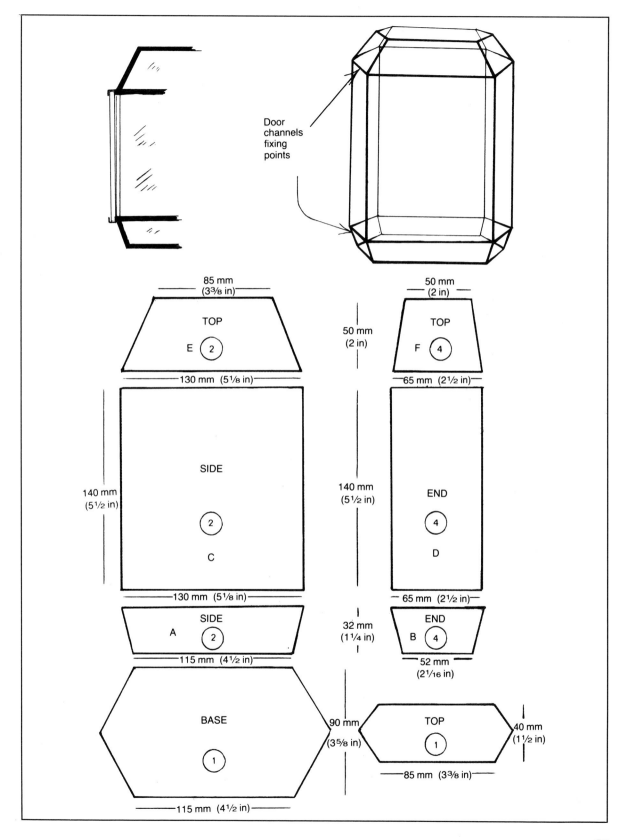

Door
channels
fixing
points

85 mm
(3⅜ in)

TOP

E ②

130 mm (5⅛ in)

SIDE

②

C

130 mm (5⅛ in)

SIDE

A ②

115 mm (4½ in)

BASE

①

115 mm (4½ in)

50 mm
(2 in)

TOP

F ④

65 mm (2½ in)

END

④

D

65 mm (2½ in)

END

B ④

52 mm
(2¹⁄₁₆ in)

50 mm
(2 in)

140 mm
(5½ in)

32 mm
(1¼ in)

140 mm
(5½ in)

140 mm
(5½ in)

90 mm
(3⅝ in)

TOP

①

85 mm (3⅜ in)

40 mm
(1½ in)

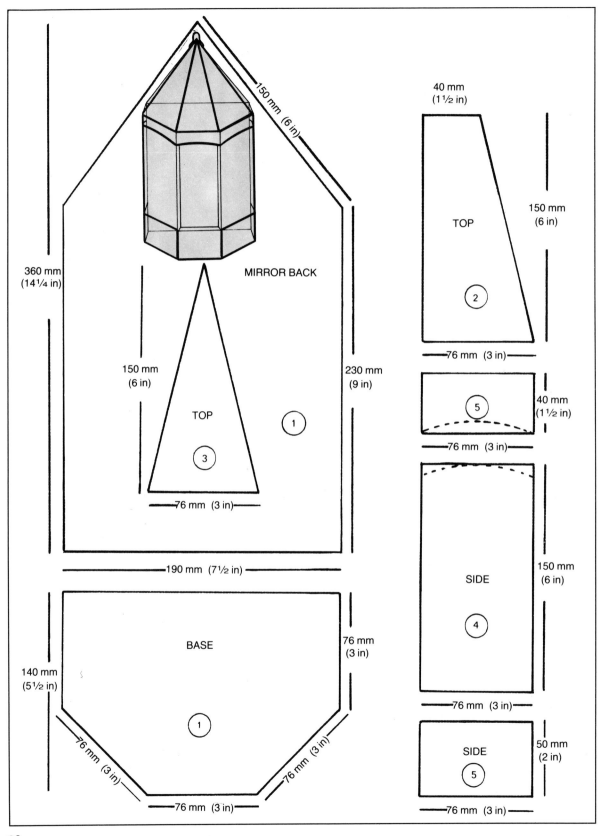

MIRROR BACK

150 mm (6 in)

360 mm (14¼ in)

230 mm (9 in)

150 mm (6 in)

TOP

1

3

76 mm (3 in)

190 mm (7½ in)

BASE

76 mm (3 in)

140 mm (5½ in)

1

76 mm (3 in)

76 mm (3 in)

76 mm (3 in)

40 mm (1½ in)

TOP

150 mm (6 in)

2

76 mm (3 in)

5

40 mm (1½ in)

76 mm (3 in)

SIDE

150 mm (6 in)

4

76 mm (3 in)

SIDE

50 mm (2 in)

5

76 mm (3 in)

MIRRORBACK (FIG. 47)

Clear Glass – 1470 cm^2 (1½ sq. ft)
Mirror Glass – 360 × 180 mm (14 × 7 in)
Solder – 0.5 kg (1 lb)
Copperfoil – ⅔ roll (22 m or 24 yd)

Method of Construction

This is fully described in Chapter 4.

Fig. 47 (Opposite)
Mirrorback.

6 Planting

A true terrarium is an enclosed glass structure, similar to a bottle garden in many ways, and a planter is a plant holder that is exposed to the atmosphere. Atlhough this may sound a rather simplistic explanation, it is important to define the two when contemplating which plants and compost to use, and the way that the plants are watered and generally taken care of.

There are many advantages in using a terrarium. The most significant is that if the proper balance of water is established when it is first planted, it will become virtually self-watering, as Dr Ward discovered over one hundred years ago. Attention should only be required two or three times a year. With modern central heating systems, a terrarium can protect plants from fluctuations in temperature caused by the heating being turned off at night, and also from changes in the weather and seasons, in unheated and exposed places.

As the plants can be left for long periods without attention, this can be an advantage when the holiday season comes around. There is no need to impose on the neighbours. Plants are also protected from draughts that can be harmful to them, causing buds and leaves to drop. The plants are shielded from dust which can clog the leaves of some species, as well as from gas and tobacco fumes. If the plants and compost have been selected with care they will remain free from the seasonal insect pests that can occur. One advantage over the conventional bottle garden is that terrariums are far easier to plant, alleviating the need for cumbersome long-handled forks and pieces of looped wire. Another problem with bottle gardens is that it is normally a disadvantage to place flowering houseplants in them as it is difficult to remove any dead flowerheads, which will eventually rot and cause problems. With a terrarium, any dead material can easily be removed. Also, if the plant looks unattractive when the flowering period is over, it can be removed and replaced with another variety. Terrarium gardening is true miniature gardening under glass.

The main disadvantage of the terrarium is that if it is over-watered it will constantly mist up. This is not only annoying but it can also be harmful to the plants, causing them to rot at their bases. If, after initial watering and planting, the terrarium does mist up simply open the door and allow the compost to dry out a little. Close the door again and, by trial and error, a correct balance can be established. This is achieved when just a faint mist appears on the inside of the glass as the temperature drops at night.

All terrariums need good drainage. Hortag and charcoal help with this.

Careful planting can create beautiful effects.

Another problem that can occur is that, as the growing conditions are so ideal, the terrarium, if wrongly positioned, will cause the plants to grow too quickly and rapidly overcrowd it. The ideal place is in good, natural light, but away from direct sunlight which should be avoided as it can heat up the interior and rapidly dry out the compost and the plants.

The doors in terrariums can be left open or omitted altogether. Although many of the advantages of the totally enclosed structure are lost, it can certainly be a help not to have a door when using trailing plants such as variegated ivy, creeping fig or tradescantia. It is sometimes of benefit to go for a compromise and build a terrarium with an opening large enough to trail plants from, but narrow enough to help retain moisture. If building a terrarium of this sort, do remember to leave the opening big enough to get a hand inside to allow for planting.

Planters, on the other hand, have no secret properties; they are merely attractive plant holders and accordingly when planted they should be treated in the same way as the humble plant pot.

COMPOSTS

It is helpful when planting terrariums to use either a sterilised loam- or a peat-based compost as opposed to garden soil. These have the advantage of being free from weeds and soil-borne diseases. Compost is more than just a medium to anchor plants; it provides reserves of food and moisture. Both types have advantages and drawbacks, some of which are detailed below.

Loam-based

John Innes is a loam-based compost, made to a specification laid down by the John Innes Institute. It is made by many manufacturers and is not a brand name. There are two types, seed and potting. The potting compost is available in three strengths, Numbers 1, 2 and 3. The basic structure of sterilised loam, granular peat and coarse sand remains the same in all three, but the amount of added fertiliser differs. Number 2 contains twice as much fertiliser as Number 1 and Number 3 contains three times as much. Number 2 is generally the most suitable for houseplants grown in terrariums and planters. One of its main advantages over peat-based compost is that it has a far better reservoir of plant food. It is also easier to judge when watering is required and this compost is more difficult to over-water. However, one of the disadvantages is that it is extremely heavy. This can be an important factor when transporting it and should also be considered when planting hanging structures that have delicate hooks to suspend them from. Loam-based composts have a tendency to dry out more quickly, although they will retain some moisture, unlike peat.

Peat-based

There are many peat-based composts available. Some manufacturers produce different seed and potting varieties, but it is best to obtain a multi-purpose type. Peat-based composts are lighter to carry than loam-based products and they are more pleasant to handle and easier to use. A further advantage is that they need watering at less frequent intervals, although it is more difficult to judge visually when watering is required. It is better to touch the compost and ensure that it stays damp, but not saturated, at all times. Once it does dry out it can be very difficult to moisten it completely again. Plants that are grown in peat-based composts need feeding at an earlier stage than those raised in loam-based composts. Most houseplants grow well in either peat or loam, but ferns, palms and mosses seem to prefer being grown in peat. Peat has a rich, dark colour that provides a beautiful contrast to the greens of the foliage in many plants.

When using either compost, a layer of drainage material about 2.5–3 cm (1–1½ in) thick should be placed in the base of the structure before adding compost and plants. Small pebbles about 5 mm (¼ in) are ideal, or hortag can be used. This is a light aggregate material which is artificially produced and is readily available from garden centres. If a terrarium is being planted it is best to mix some wood charcoal with the drainage material. This acts as a filter and keeps the compost sweet. Do not be tempted to use barbecue charcoal as this has special additives to help it burn and these are harmful to plants.

CHOOSING PLANTS

When choosing plants it is a good plan to have some idea of their rate of growth. This cannot be an exact science since it obviously depends on temperature and where they are situated, but it is helpful to try to visualise the plant layout in, say, six months' time.

Allow sufficient space for the plants to grow. There is nothing worse than a terrarium packed out with plants. If the layout does look a little sparse at first, fill the empty spaces with rocks, stones or pebbles. A small rockery makes an interesting feature and a natural-looking addition as the plants begin to grow over and around it. Cork bark is an easily obtainable material. Often used for dried flower arrangements, it can provide a neutral background against which to display climbing plants such as the ivies and creeping figs. It can also be broken into small pieces and used as a rockery. Other space fillers are the many varieties of moss. Terrariums are miniature gardens under glass and should be cultivated as such.

It is better to arrange the compost in a sloping or undulating manner. Plant the tallest varieties of plants at the back with smaller plants progressing towards the front. Choose small, sturdy, healthy plants, even though a lot of time may be spent in looking for the right ones. Supermarkets and garden centres are good sources, as their turnover is normally high and stocks are constantly being replaced. It is best to avoid shops and market stalls that display houseplants outside, especially in winter. If plants are purchased in winter they should be carefully wrapped in a couple of sheets of newspaper or some other form of protection to shield them from harmful draughts on the journey home.

Fig. 48 Asparagus plumosus.

Reject any that have faded or drooping leaves. Carefully examine the plants for signs of disease and insect pests before buying. When looking for plants that are to be cultivated in a terrarium, it is alway best to try to find the smallest possible; many garden centres have a special selection of bottle garden plants.

SOME SUITABLE HOUSEPLANTS
Asparagus

Asparagus is often wrongly described as a fern. It is in fact an ornamental form of the well known edible species. There are many forms although only two species seem available as houseplants.

Asparagus plumosus (Fig. 48) has a deep green feathery foliage which has a light delicate look. The shape is, in some ways, reminiscent of the Cedar of Lebanon Tree (*Cedrus libani*). It makes an attractive centrepiece for planting displays with smaller plants arranged below it. Under normal conditions it reaches a height of about 23 cm (10 in).

(Opposite) A miniature herb garden. Note the etched glass Mint label.

Fig. 49 Asparagus sprengeri.

Asparagus sprengeri (Fig. 49) is an entirely different plant. Normally used as a trailing plant, it has green spiky leaves and is often used in cut flower arrangements.

Both of these species can be grown from seed and a number of well known seed merchants have them in their catalogues. Best planted in the spring, they take between 21 and 35 days to germinate in a temperature of 18–21°C (65–70°F). They are slow-growing and take about two years to reach a useful height. *Asparagus* requires good light but not direct sunlight and needs to be well watered.

Begonia

Opinions differ as to where the foliage *Begonia* originated; some say the Himalayas, others the forest of Assam in India. The *Begonia rex* varieties have been widely hybridised since their introduction over 130 years ago. The lop-sided heart-shaped leaves are produced in many colour combinations.

Begonia metallica has a rather metallic sheen to its leaves. These have purplish veins running through them.

Begonia masoniana is a very popular plant. It is often called the Iron Cross Begonia as it has a bold chocolate brown marking on the green leaves similar to the pattern of an iron cross. There are so many variations that it is best left to individual choice.

Begonias enjoy a humid atmosphere and plenty of light. They are happy in any soil, although some seem to prefer soil-less composts. It must be free-draining. Begonias can easily be grown from seed; however, the minute seeds need careful handling and must not be covered with compost. Sow from mid-winter onwards. Germinate in a temperature of 18–24°C (65–75°F) which takes about 14–28 days.

Campanula isophylla

This is a favourite for hanging planters. *Campanula isophylla*, or the Italian Bellflower, is a perennial and does originate from Italy. Although there are nearly 300 different *Campanula* varieties, only a few are grown as houseplants. The foliage has trailing stems and long grey-green toothed leaves. These are approximately 2.5–4 cm (1–1½ in) long. The plant is covered with a profusion of tiny, fine-pointed star-like blooms. *Campanula isophylla alba* has tiny white flowers, and *Campanula isophylla* 'Mayii' rather longer pale blue flowers.

Campanula need a bright airy position, and should be watered freely, and any dead flowerheads should be removed to help invigorate the rest of the plant. Care should be taken when moving the plant as the stems are very brittle and can break easily. There are three methods of propagation. Seed can be sown in early spring in about a 16°C (60°F) temperature; the plants can be divided as new growth begins; or cuttings may be taken.

Ceropegia linearis woodii

This trailing plant is commonly called String of Hearts or Rosary Vine. The first name is an apt description. The plant has the appearance of a thick piece of string with heart-shaped dark green leaves clinging to it. These leaves have a grey mottled finish to them. Although normally a trailing plant it can be made to climb up trellises or pieces of bark. Originally from Zimbabwe, *Ceropegia linearis woodii* needs reasonable light to survive and must have a well-drained soil with average room temperature.

Propagation is by stem cuttings. These should be taken when the plant is resting. They should be allowed to dry out for a couple of days and then be placed in either a sandy soil or tepid water.

Chlorophytum (Fig. 50)

This easily-grown trailing foliage plant is a must for hanging planters. The Spider Plant, as it is commonly known, originates from South Africa. It has narrow, rush-like green leaves which have a creamy stripe running down the middle. In summer long stems grow from the centre of the plant and bear small green and white star-shaped plantlets, an exact miniature of the mother plant. These can be pressed into pots of compost while they are still attached to the main plant and left to root. As the tiny

Fig. 50 Chlorophytum
(Spider Plant).

plant begins to grow more leaves, the stem joining the two plants may be cut. The Spider Plant is one of the easiest houseplants to grow. It enjoys a humid atmosphere and is very tolerant of low temperatures. However, chills and draughts can cause yellowing to the tips of the leaves. It is not very fussy about light conditions but direct sunlight should be avoided.

Codiaeum variegatum

Codiaeum, or more popularly Joseph's Coat, originates from Malaysia, Sri Lanka, Java and India. It has glossy, rather leathery leaves, multi-coloured in vivid shades of green, yellow, orange, pink, crimson and brown. This houseplant is often a challenge to cultivate successfully as it needs constant warmth and good humidity. It dislikes cool and draughty places. This makes it a natural choice for the enclosed environment of a terrarium. *Codiaeum* needs good light and will even tolerate full sunlight for limited periods. Poor light will cause the variegated leaves to turn green. Plants should be obtained from a reliable source. It is best not to buy plants that have been left outside or not properly looked after. Propagation is by stem cuttings, but is best left to experts.

Ficus (Figs)

The *Ficus* genus has many well-known and impressive foliage plants.

Fig. 51 Ficus pumila
(Creeping Fig).

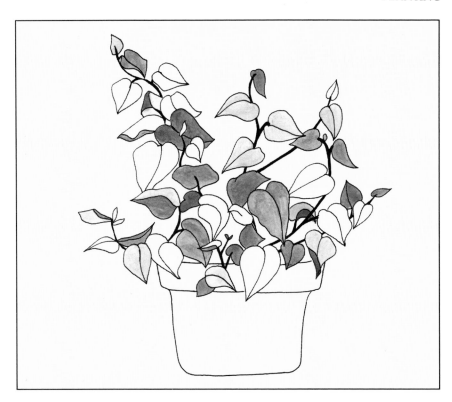

These include some very large varieties. *Ficus elastica*, the Rubber Plant, is a familiar sight in homes and offices.

Ficus pumila (Fig. 51), however, is a different matter. Commonly known as the Creeping Fig, it has an abundance of tiny heart-shaped leaves that grow to approximately 2.5 cm (1 in) across. The plant is easy to grow, is tolerant of low temperatures and enjoys humid conditions. As such it is an ideal choice for terrariums and planters. The Creeping Fig gives out aerial roots and is a natural climber or trailer. If it is over-watered its leaves tend to turn yellow.

Ficus radicans is another climber of the fig family. It has oblong spear-shaped leaves that are approximately 5 cm (2 in) long. The variegated variety is very attractive with its green and cream leaves.

Both of these figs are useful plants for terrariums. They require well-drained soil and reasonable light.

Fittonia

Fittonia originates from Peru and Brazil. The Latin name is taken from Sarah and Elizabeth Fitton who were joint authors of a book entitled *Botanical Conversations. Fittonia* is sometimes called the Hieroglyphic Plant. Two species are grown as houseplants.

Fittonia argyroneura (Fig. 52), is more commonly known as the Snakeskin or Lace Leaf plant. It is a beautiful trailing plant with oval leaves about 10 cm (4 in) long, bright green in colour with pale silvery veins.

Fittonia gigantea is a small shrub which can reach a height of 45 cm (18

Fig. 52 Fittonia argyroneura *(Snakeskin or Lace Leaf Plant).*

Fig. 53 Hedera helix sagittaefolia *'Glacier'.*

in). The leaves have crimson-coloured veins. It is unsuitable for cold places where humidity is low and temperatures tend to fluctuate, so is therefore an ideal choice for terrariums. It also tolerates poor lighting conditions and is quite happy growing in shady corners.

Hedera

The ivies are a very useful group of foliage plants. They can be grown as climbers or trailing plants. Many of the ivies are cultivars of the English or Common Ivy *Hedera helix.* There are many varieties with different leaf shapes. For terrariums it is best to concentrate on the many small-leaved types.

Hedera helix sagittaefolia (Fig. 53) has attractive green star-shaped leaves. 'Glacier' is light and dark green with creamy-yellow patches around the edges of the leaves. 'Little Diamond' has mid-green leaves with white borders.

Hedera canariensis 'Variegata' (Fig. 54) is rather different from the smaller types. The Canary Islands Ivy is a bigger plant altogether. Its leaves are 7–10 cm (3–4 in) long with a spear-shaped pattern. They have irregular markings of light and dark green.

Ivies are easy to grow outdoors, but indoors they are best kept in cool conditions. If the air becomes too dry they can suffer attack from red spider mite. When kept in a warm atmosphere they can grow vigorously.

Fig. 54 Hedera canariensis *'Variegata' (Canary Islands Ivy).*

Ivies can be cut back at any time, although it is best to do this in the spring. Propagation is easily achieved by taking small cuttings in summer and placing them in a small container of peat-based compost. Ivies enjoy a humid atmosphere and are quite tolerant to temperature changes. The small variegated types can be grown successfully in bathrooms.

Helxine soleirolii

Commonly known as Baby's Tears or Mind Your Own Business, this plant originally comes from the islands of Corsica and Sardinia. The plant forms a dense mass of tiny leaves that creep and trail over everything in its path. It has for many years been used for ground cover in greenhouses. This plant is an ideal choice for a terrarium as it flourishes in humid conditions. It is very useful for planting around miniature rockeries. Once it is established it will grow very rapidly.

There are three different leaf colourings. The original species has a mid-green colouring, 'Aurea' has a bright, golden colour, and 'Argentia' has tiny silver leaves. Propagation is best achieved by dividing the plants in the spring. Soil for successful growing should be moist but well-drained. These plants can tolerate partial shade and fairly low temperatures. When transferring the plant from the pot to the terrarium, care should be taken as it has a very shallow root structure which can be damaged if it is mishandled.

(Opposite) A large Diamond Planter finished in black patina planted up with Asparagus Fern (Asparagus Plumosa), Polka Dot Plant (Hypoestus), Pilea and Fittonia.

Fig. 55 Hypoestus (Polka Dot Plant).

Hypoestus

Hypoestus or the Polka Dot Plant (Fig. 55) originates from Madagascar and has become very popular as a houseplant during the past few years. The leaves, which are a dark olive green and oblong in shape, are speckled with bright pink patches. The amount of colour in the leaves can vary from individual batches of seed. When bought, it is best to pinch out the growing tips to encourage a bushy plant. If this is not done the plants can become very straggly and untidy. If the plant is happy with its conditions, it will flower with tiny purple and white blooms, although this takes some time to achieve. Hypoestus needs good light but not direct sunlight. It is a very easy plant to grow and will add contrast when planted against a background of green foliage plants. It enjoys humidity and grows well in terrariums. Propagation can be made by cuttings taken in the spring, although they are quite easy to grow from seed. Seed grown in early spring will produce presentable plants by the summer. Germination takes 14–28 days in a temperature of 16–18°C (60–65°F).

Maranta

Maranta is a member of the Arrowroot family and comes from tropical America. The Latin name comes from the Venetian botanist Bartolomeo Maranti, circa 1550.

It is an attractive foliage houseplant that is suitable for terrariums as it enjoys humid conditions, although it should be allowed drier ones during the winter period. A *Maranta* that is widely grown is *Maranta leuconeura* and its cultivars. Commonly known as the Prayer Plant, because it has a curious habit of closing its leaves together and holding them erect during the evening, it has large oval leaves which can grow up to 15 cm (6 in) wide. They are a mixture of mid-green and light green stripes with dark brown ribs running from the middle. The undersides of the leaves are a reddish brown. They should be grown in good light out of direct sunlight. Drainage is important and should be of sufficient depth to provide free-draining soil. Propagation is by dividing the rhizome with a sharp knife and re-potting it in the spring.

Mimosa pudica

Mimosa, or the Sensitive Plant, as it is more commonly known, is a rather unimpressive little plant. It has a woody, rather spindly stem. The feathery oblong green leaves fold inwards when they are touched or shaken, which gives it its name. A sharp vibration can also cause the plant to collapse and look as though it has wilted. After a while, however, the branches revive and attain their original shape. Although it is not the most impressive houseplant, it should certainly be grown for its curiosity value.

Being small it is an ideal space filler for terrariums. It can be grown in light conditions ranging from semi-shade to semi-sun and should be kept evenly moist. *Mimosa* is an easy plant to raise from seed, which should be sown in spring in a temperature of 18–21°C (65–70°F). The seeds take

14–21 days to germinate. If the seeds do not germinate it may help to soak them in tepid water overnight before sowing. Prick them out into 7.5 cm (3 in) pots when they are big enough to handle and then transfer them again to their final position when they are growing well.

Peperomia

These attractive foliage plants can be grown very successfully in terrariums. There are nearly 1,000 species in this genus. They originate from many tropical and semi-tropical areas.

Peperomia argyreia is often called the Watermelon Peperomia, and has its origins in Brazil. It has dark green oval leaves which have strips of silver in them.

Peperomia caperata has a large number of dark green velvety leaves that have a deep corrugated appearance. It is commonly known as the Emerald Ripple.

Peperomia griseoargentea is a beautiful variety which has silver and green variegated, velvety leaves.

Peperomia should be grown in good light, and should be watered with care, enjoying a fairly dry soil. Ensure that the soil is free-draining by placing plenty of pebbles or drainage material over the base of the terrarium before planting. Propagation is by taking stem cuttings in the spring, and placing them in sandy soil which must be kept cool but not too moist.

Fig. 56 Pilea cadierei *(Aluminium Plant).*

Pilea

There are almost 400 species of *Pilea*, of which a few are grown commercially as houseplants.

Pilea cadierei, the Aluminium Plant (Fig. 56), is a very popular, attractive foliage plant. It has deep green leaves, spotted with a shiny silver patina. It has a compact bushy shape and can grow to a height of 30 cm (12 in).

Pilea nummulariifolia, known as the Artillery Plant or Pistol Plant, is a beautiful bushy plant with a ferny type of foliage. It can be grown outdoors and reaches a height of about 15 cm (6 in). From late spring to early autumn tiny green-yellow flowers appear. On the slightest touch they issue clouds of pollen into the air, giving the plants their common name.

Pilea need plenty of light and not too much heat. They should be watered sparingly, as too much water can cause the stems to rot and the plant will lose its leaves. If the plant grows too straggly it is best to take out the growing tips, causing new shoots to appear at the base and improve the shape. Propagation is best achieved by taking cuttings in mid-spring or by sowing seeds in a warm greenhouse in early spring.

Saintpaulia

The African Violet has become a very popular houseplant in recent years. It comes from East Africa where it was discovered in 1892 by Baron Walter von Saint Paul who was governor of German East Africa at that time. It is easy to grow, and if reasonable care is taken the plant will last a long time. The plant has no main stem; it does in fact grow from a central rosette-shaped crown. The oblong, heart-shaped leaves are various shades of green. It flowers in summer; but, if grown in the proper conditions, it can also flower in the winter, sometimes flowering twice a year.

Saintpaulia ionantha grows to about 10 cm (4 in) high with attractive vivid purple-blue flowers with golden yellow eyes.

Saintpaulia variegata has attractive variegated white and yellow leaves.

Saintpaulia tongwensis is very similar to *Saintpaulia ionantha* but with much longer leaves shaded with a purple and bronze tint; the flowers are a vivid purple and have wrinkled petals.

The secret of successfully growing African Violets is careful watering. The ideal source is rain water. If planted in a terrarium, the humidity should be kept fairly low. They should be placed in a good light. If it is too intense the leaves have a tendency to turn yellow. African Violets can be easily grown from seed. They are best sown in spring or early summer. The seeds should be placed on top of the compost and a polythene bag placed over them to conserve moisture. Germinate in a temperature of 21–24°C (70–75°F). It can take 21–42 days for the seedlings to appear.

Sansevieria trifasciata

Sansevieria trifasciata is sometimes called the Snake Plant or, more unkindly, Mother-In-Law's Tongue. It takes its name from the eighteenth-

(Opposite) Mirrorback with variegated Ivy (Hedera) and Aluminium Plant (Pilea).

110

century Prince of Sansevieria (Raimond de Sango) who was born in Naples in 1710.

The Snake Plant is a very easy plant to grow and only prolonged neglect will harm it. The leaves are long and narrow and sword-like with very pointed ends. The mottled green colour and texture of the leaves is very reminiscent of a snake. The leaves have a bright yellow border around them and stick up from the soil in clumps.

Sansevieria hahnii is entirely different. It is a low-growing plant with rosette-shaped clumps of shorter, oval leaves. These are dark green and mottled with grey.

Either species will grow well in a peat-based compost. They should be watered regularly during the growing period from early spring to early autumn. Provide the plant with good light but keep it away from direct sunlight as this can easily scorch the leaves. There are two ways to propagate. The most usual method is to divide the plant cutting it with a sharp knife. This is best carried out during summer when the plant is growing vigorously. The other way is by leaf cuttings. Cut a leaf close to the base, divide the leaf into 4.5 cm (3 in) pieces and push them into compost. This is best carried out in the spring.

Selaginella

Selaginella, like *Asparagus*, is often referred to as a fern. They are in fact from the Selaginellaceae family and are found in many parts of tropical America and Australia. They are tiny upright climbing plants, similar in many ways to moss in appearance. Like moss, it thrives in a humid atmosphere, but does not like a very damp soil. It is an ideal plant to grow with ferns as they enjoy the same sort of environment. This is another plant that, like *Helxine soleirolii*, looks attractive when planted near a miniature rockery. There are numerous attractive varieties, ranging from yellow to mid-green leaf colourings. Propagation is by division which is best achieved in the spring.

Streptocarpus hybridus

The Cape Primrose is a native of South Africa and Madagascar. It was brought to England in 1826 when it was first grown at Kew Gardens in October of that year. The Cape Primrose is from the same family as the African Violet and should be grown under the same conditions. The flowers are trumpet-like in appearance and the plant usually produces blooms from late spring until autumn, or even later if conditions are favourable.

As with African Violets, it is important to pinch out any dead flowerheads. The Cape Primrose is a stemless plant with a bunch of long green leaves which have a rather waxy appearance. There are many hybrids of *streptocarpus hybridus*. These include 'Constant Nymph' which has blue and purple flowers, 'Rexii', a delicate powder blue with white in the throat of the trumpet, and 'Karen', a magenta and dark pink.

The Cape Primrose is easy to grow and needs to be kept evenly moist in reasonable light but not direct sunlight. Care should be taken with the foliage as it can be rather brittle. They can be raised from seed and many leading seed merchants offer some beautiful varieties. They should be sown in the autumn using a peat-based compost. Care should be taken not to cover the seeds which are very small. Germinate in a temperature of 18–24°C (65–75°F). This takes 14–21 days. Propagation can also be achieved by taking leaf cuttings from early to mid-summer. The leaf should be cut into small pieces and placed in the compost and left to rest in a temperature of about 18°C (65°F). A polythene bag should be placed over the pot to maintain humidity.

Tradescantia

This attractive plant is extremely easy to grow and propagate. Its Latin name derives from John Tradescant who was employed as a gardener by Charles I. He brought the plant to England from Virginia. If you should be in Hertfordshire, England, try to find time to visit Hatfield House where on the newel post at the bottom of the main staircase you will see the head of John Tradescant carved. The plant's common name is Wandering Jew.

Mainly a trailing plant, there are many different varieties. They have enlarged leaves, some with coloured stripes splashed across them. If a more bushy plant is required, the growing tips can be pinched out as they appear in the spring. Some of the decorative varieties are as follows.

Tradescantia fluminensis 'Quicksilver' has elongated mid-green leaves with silvery grey stripes.

Tradescantia albiflora has tiny white butterfly-shaped flowers which only last for a day, with green leaves.

Tradescantia fluminensis 'Tricolour' has long spear-shaped leaves with green, purple and white stripes on them.

Tradescantia need good light to preserve the variegation in the leaves. An occasional misting with water can also be beneficial. They can be propagated by division which is best carried out in the spring, although cuttings can be taken at any time by planting in a sandy compost.

Zebrina

Zebrina, or the Inch Plant to give it its common name, is a native of Mexico. Its Latin name refers to the stripes on its oval-shaped leaves. It is a trailing foliage plant that is often confused with *Tradescantia*, having a similar appearance, although its leaves are sometimes slightly larger. As with *Tradescantia*, there are many varieties with some very decorative stripes.

Zebrina pendula has green leaves that have two silvery grey bands running across them.

Zebrina pendula 'Prupussi' the Bronze Inch Plant, has purple and olive green striping above the leaf and a bright purple colouring underneath. Growing conditions are the same as for *Tradescantia* (see above) which also applies to the propagation methods.

Ferns

Ferns have been used as attractive houseplants for many hundreds of years, but their history goes back much further than that. There are many species of fern; some 9,000 varieties are believed to exist. They flourish from north of the Arctic Circle and are found at altitudes of over 4,500 m (15,000 feet) in the Himalayas. The fern is an ancient plant, which has been growing on the earth for many thousands of years. During the carboniferous period it provided a great deal of the vegetable matter that was compressed to form the coal that we use today. The fern does not flower, but its beauty lies in the many different leaf colours and shapes. They make an ideal background for the more colourful plants such as the African Violet or *Begonia rex*. Ferns became very popular in Victorian times due, in part, to the invention by Dr Ward of his Wardian case, although they were grown in earlier times in lean-to greenhouses without any openings, which were known as ferneries.

A fern is an ideal subject for terrariums, as they are reasonably slow-growing and enjoy a moist, humid atmosphere, although they do not enjoy a waterlogged soil. A well drained soil-less compost is ideal. The soil should be kept sweet by adding wood charcoal to the drainage material or as a separate layer placed on top of it. The compost should never be allowed to dry out. A regular misting of tepid water using a hand sprayer will help to keep the foliage in good condition. It is also a good idea to spray them occasionally with a foliar feed. Ferns can tolerate poor light conditions, although it is best if they are grown in reasonable light but not direct sunlight as this can burn the leaves. Propagation can be achieved by planting spores, but this is best left to experts. A far more reliable method is by dividing the plant at the end of the winter before it begins to grow again.

Some easily grown ferns are the following.

Adiantum cuneatum, the Maidenhair Fern (Fig. 57), is a delicate-looking fern which originates from Central America. It has thousands of tiny light green leaves that are supported by long thin, wire-like stems.

Pellaea rotundifolia, the Button Fern (Fig. 58), originates from New Zealand, and has a rather flat and compact growth pattern. The narrow fronds have small circular leaves which are a glossy dark green, supported by thin wiry stems. It is an easy plant to grow, but unlike most ferns it does not enjoy high humidity, so hand-misting is not advisable. The Button Fern will tolerate shady conditions.

Phyllitis Scolopendrium, the Hart's Tongue Fern, is a native of North America. It is a hardy easy-to-grow plant which has long strap-like leaves with wavy edges, which are a glossy bright green. Some plants grow as many as fifty leaves from the central growing tuft. Being hardy, it is best kept fairly cool. Regular mist spraying is a help in keeping this fern in good condition.

The *Pteris* group of ferns need warm conditions to flourish. None of them are hardy, unlike the Hart's Tongue Fern. Commonly known as Ribbon Ferns, they have delicate ribbon-type pointed leaves. There are

Fig. 57 Adiantum
(Maidenhair Fern).

Fig. 58 Pellaea rotundifolia.
(Button Fern)

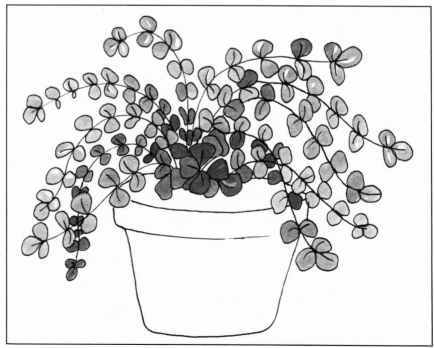

many varieties, some having striped variegated leaves. Two particularly attractive varieties are *Pteris ensitormis* 'Victoriae' (Fig. 59), which has slender grey and green fronds, and *Pteris cretica* 'Wilsonii' which has bright green foliage and crested tips to the fronds. As they enjoy a humid atmosphere *Pteris* ferns are an ideal choice for bathrooms and kitchens.

There are many cultivars of *Nephrolepsis*. One of the most popular is *Nephrolepsis exaltata*, the Ladder Fern, with its long green leaves that look like attractive plumes growing from the centre of the plant. *N. exaltata* 'Bostoniansis', the Boston Fern, is another easily-managed variety.

Platycerium bifurcatum, the Stagshorn Fern, is an unusual fern that is a native of Australia and New Guinea. It often grows on the trunks of trees. The fronds have an antler-like appearance, giving the plant its common name. The Stagshorn Fern is best grown vertically, allowing the fronds to hang down. Being from a tropical climate it does need a little different treatment. Instead of ordinary compost it should be grown in a container firmly packed with sphagnum moss. It is best to add a little bonemeal and charcoal to the moss before the fern is planted. Regular spraying with tepid water will help the plant to thrive.

Palms

Palms were another favourite plant often found in the Victorian drawing room along with the ferns and the ever-faithful *Aspidistra*. Today their graceful shapes and soothing green shades help to decorate many a home or office.

Fig. 59 Pteris ensitormis 'Victoriae'.

Fig. 60 Chamaedora elegans *(Parlour Palm).*

Most palms are far too big to be accommodated in anything but the largest terrarium. However, *Chamaedorea elegans*, more popularly known as the Parlour Palm (Fig. 60), is an exception. The seed for the Parlour Palm is produced in many parts of the world and small plants of about a year old are widely available. They are slow-growing and make an ideal choice for miniature gardening under glass. The Parlour Palm makes a good companion to the many types of fern available as they enjoy similar conditions. If it should outgrow its environment it can easily be removed, re-potted and grown on elsewhere.

Mosses

In a terrarium moss can be used as an ideal medium to cover the compost with a bright green living carpet. It is often difficult to grow mosses indoors as they need to be kept in humid conditions. They tend to dry out quickly if they are not frequently sprayed with water, but this is of course no problem in the terrarium.

There was a time in the Victorian era when moss gardens became popular. In Japan they have been a traditional form of gardening for many hundreds of years. Mosses can look particularly attractive if planted with ferns as they are often found growing in woods and beside streams in the wild, together. Another advantage of using mosses is that they can tolerate shady conditions.

Mosses can be found in many places: in woods around the roots of trees, beside streams, on garden paths and along the sides of shady lanes, in fact anywhere where there are humid shady conditions. When collecting moss it is best if it can be lifted gently in one piece as if lifting a carpet. Although they have simple stems and leaves, they have no real root structure. Mosses are attached to their growing position by rhizoids, which are small colourless hairlike roots. After collecting moss it is a good idea to place it in a polythene bag to retain moisture and stop it drying out. Keep it in the bag in a cool place until the moss is to be used.

Herbs

A herb is usually considered to be a plant with healing or aromatic properties. Herbs have been enjoying a renewed popularity during recent years. They add flavour and a dash of elegance and sophistication to very ordinary meals. Most are obtained in dehydrated form from the supermarket or health food shop, and it is a surprise to many people that herbs can be grown on a sunny windowsill. Many of the smaller varieties of culinary herbs such as chives, parsley and thyme can be grown easily in a terrarium or even a large glass bottle, many of them from seed.

Indoor herb gardening has many advantages. Not only are the plants decorative but they can also be freshly picked and used when they are required. This is a real bonus for the flat dweller or for anyone without a garden.

Herbs are a delight to grow as most of them only require three things: a soil that is not too rich, plenty of sunshine, and moisture. Ordinary compost, either John Innes No. 2 or soil-less compost, is suitable. Charcoal should be added, as well as a good drainage material such as pebbles or pea gravel. If the soil is too rich the plants will have large leaves but lack flavour and fragrance. If this does happen change the compost to a mixture of 50 per cent sifted garden soil and 50 per cent compost. Add the charcoal and drainage material as before. The plants tend to sulk if they are left standing in waterlogged soil. Turn the plants around every few days to stop them growing towards the light.

Ocimum basilicum (Sweet Basil)

Basil is a spicy-tasting herb with a slight peppery taste, useful for green salads or flavouring sauces, egg, fish and especially tomato and pasta dishes. Being an annual it is best grown from seed in the spring. The seeds are easy to germinate and the plant grows to a height of 30–60 cm (1–2 ft). The leaves are varying shades of green and purple with minute white flowers. Basil loves a sunny windowsill and is unhappy in anything but full sun. Pinch out the growing tip to encourage bushy growth. The best time to harvest is just as the buds are beginning to open. Basil is at its best when picked young and it is often better to make successive sowings.

Allium schoenoprasum (Chives)

Chives (Fig. 61) are one of the easiest grown plants for the kitchen herb

(Opposite) Mirrorback constructed with opalescent glass.

Fig. 61 Allium schoenoprasum *(Chives).*

garden. They germinate easily from seed and grow quite well on a sunny windowsill. They grow in grasslike clumps of 23–60 cm (9–24 in) in height. The flowers have an attractive lavender colour. As soon as the foliage is long enough it can be harvested. Cut about 2.5–5 cm (1–2 in) off the tips using a pair of scissors. The leaves are best cut in the morning when the aromatic oils are high in the plant's leaves. The clipped leaves will continue to grow on a 'cut and come again' basis.

The leaves have a mild onion flavour and can be used for soups, salads, cheese and egg dishes. The plant can be divided in the autumn and potted on for use during the winter. The leaves can also be cut in the morning on a hot sunny day and left to dry, after which they should be stored in an airtight container.

Mentha spp. (Mint)

Mint is another perennial, which grows 30–90 cm (1–3 ft) high. There are many varieties, of which spearmint is the most popular, although there are many others such as peppermint, orangemint and applemint. Leaf colouring varies from dark green to green streaked with purple and yellow. There is an attractive variegated variety with green and cream edged leaves. The flowers are always purple. Mint is best grown from cuttings. Simply place the stem in water in a sunny position. As the roots

Fig. 62 Petroselinum crispum *(Parsley).*

begin to develop, transfer the plant to the position where it is to grow.

The big problem with mint is not in encouraging it to grow but trying to stop it. It is best planted in a container on its own. Mint grows well on any windowsill in either sunlight or shade as long as it is kept close to the glass where the light is strongest. Traditionally used as a sauce mixed with vinegar for lamb, it has many other uses. It is excellent for enlivening peas, beans and potatoes and can be made into a delicious mint tea. Chopped-up leaves can be frozen in ice cubes to give cold drinks a refreshing flavour. Mint can be preserved by either drying it in small bunches or by freezing it.

Petroselinum crispum (Parsley)

Parsley (Fig. 62) is a biennial. Although usually considered to be a garnish for fish and salad dishes, it is an important vegetable on its own. It is a rich source of Vitamin A and, if left uncooked, an excellent source of Vitamin C. The plant can either be grown from seed or obtained as a small plant from a nursery. When raised from seed it should be soaked for at least twenty-four hours before it is to be used. If seed is sown indoors in both spring and autumn, it is possible to grow parsley all year round.

The seeds take between two and four weeks to germinate. Germination being rather spasmodic, it is best to plant at least five or six seeds to ensure success. The plant takes about seventy days to grow before harvesting can take place. It grows 15–30 cm (6–12 in) high with attractive dark green leaves. Parsley has a refreshing fragrance on its own or combined with chives and spring onions.

Rosmarinus officinalis (Rosemary)

Its fragrant leaves are often used for flavouring soups, stews, fish or meat dishes. Rosemary is often referred to as the queen of herbs. It is a very ancient plant and records of its use date back some 3,000 years. It is a perennial which is best grown from either a cutting taken in autumn or a bought plant. Rosemary can be grown from seed, but germination can be a little slow and erratic.

In spring it produces a beautiful palish blue flower. Rosemary grows well in a cool sunny position and as it grows requires a fair amount of space, as it can grow up to 60 cm (24 in) high. It should be kept well pruned to encourage a more bushy plant. Apart from flavouring, rosemary is an excellent herb that can be used for making a refreshing cup of tea. Rosemary tea is very relaxing if drunk last thing at night sweetened with honey.

Cacti and Succulents

Cacti and succulents may seem a strange choice to grow in a terrarium, as they certainly do not require the humid conditions which more conventional houseplants thrive on. In fact their needs are exactly the opposite: a dry environment with plenty of light. Indeed, they grow best in direct sunlight. Cacti and succulents can, however, be grown without problems in an enclosed structure, the terrarium acting more as a display case.

The term 'succulents' describes the fleshy nature of the plant tissue, and there are a large number of species included in this group. Cacti belong to the Caraceae family, and are really only another form of succulent, but many indoor gardeners tend to elevate them into a class of their own. Succulents have one thing in common, in that they are all 'xerophilious', a term used for plants and animals that have adapted to living in dry, arid conditions. The fleshy, spongy structure of the plant means that it can retain large amounts of water.

The leaves on many succulents are very small and some plants have only stems and no leaves at all. These have many advantages: they can withstand a dry atmosphere, an important factor in many centrally-heated homes, and unlike many houseplants they do not require constant care and can be left for several weeks unattended, a useful consideration when holidays occur. A popular misconception is that succulents, and especially cacti, grow only in pure sand. This is entirely untrue. Ordinary John Innes Number 2 peat-based composts are suitable, although some enthusiasts mix one third of sharp sand or vermiculite with the standard compost to help improve the drainage.

The secret for growing succulents is to have a compost that is well drained. Succulents detest being waterlogged, which causes their roots to

Various coloured glass samples.

rot. Adding a pinch of bonemeal and some activated charcoal is also beneficial. The charcoal helps to prevent fermentation and mould-forming. Before placing the compost in the terrarium, an even layer of pea gravel or small pebbles about 5 cm (2 in) deep should be spread across the base.

The number of succulents that can be grown as houseplants is vast. It is best to obtain a suitable book for further information (see the Bibliography).

7 Dried Flowers

Dried flowers can offer an attractive and colourful alternative to normal houseplant arrangements for terrariums and planters. The enclosed glass structure of a terrarium makes an excellent display case, not only keeping the preserved flowers dust-free, but the glass also seems to magnify their delicate beauty.

Another advantage of dried flowers is that they can be used in dark places where normal plants fade and die, such as a windowless hallway or a dark corner in any room. Dried flowers are in fact best kept away from too strong a light as it fades the colour of the petals.

They often offer a far more colourful display than the various shades of green of many of the more mundane houseplants. Dried flowers make interesting table centres and brighten up gloomy alcoves. They can also look attractive when stuck onto a mirror using a few blobs of contact adhesive and arranged as a flower picture. Pressed flowers and foliage can be mounted onto paper and sandwiched between two pieces of thin glass (2 mm is ideal). The edges of the glass are foiled to seal them. The glass panel can then either be incorporated in a terrarium or planter, or a number of panels could be used to make an original trinket box. A further idea is to make a larger pressed flower panel, edge it with some pieces of attractive stained glass (fractures and streamers for instance) and use it simply as a picture.

Shops selling dried flowers seem to be few and far between, although some florists stock a limited amount of dried material. These should not be confused with the silk flowers that are often offered for sale. Silk flowers are a reasonable alternative to the dried varieties, but they should be chosen with care as many have bright, unnatural colours and lack the fragile look of dried flowers. Silk flowers can also be very expensive.

If shops for dried material can be located they usually offer a large display of flowers, leaves and flower-arranging accessories. Quite often, much of the stock is imported and when choosing a watchful eye should be kept for some of the more exotic colourings. They are frequently dyed with bright, eye-catching colours. These are often frowned upon by the more purist dried flower enthusiasts. Dried flowers, like silk ones, can be costly.

Another problem is that many dried flower outlets do not operate a mail-order service as, due to the delicate nature of the merchandise, they do not travel well, so personal shopping is essential. A far better and more interesting alternative is to dry and preserve the flowers and foliage for yourself. The tools and materials needed for drying and preserving flowers are very easy to obtain, in fact most, if not all, can be found in the average household.

Chemicals such as borax, glycerine and silica gel can easily be obtained from large chemists and are fairly inexpensive as, apart from the glycerine, they can be used over and over again.

The obvious place to start looking for the raw materials is your own garden. Even if a garden is not available, a vast range of flowers, grasses and foliage are growing wild in woods, hedgerows and round the sides of fields etc. If gathering wild material, remember to do it with care and consideration, as some plants are becoming very rare. Some species are protected by law in many parts of the world, and it is illegal to pick them. In the U.K. the Wild Flowers and Countryside Protection Act should be referred to before anything is gathered, and it is always advisable to seek expert advice.

There are a number of different methods of preserving plant material. It is best to choose one that can be used in the space and facilities that are available. Also, certain flowers and foliage require varying methods of preservation. Whichever method is finally chosen, three golden rules should be remembered when collecting materials.

1) Make sure that any materials gathered are completely free from moisture. Plants and flowers are best harvested on a warm, sunny day, never when it has recently been raining or if the plants are heavy with dew. Wet and damp plants are likely to become mildewed as the drying or preserving process takes place, causing them to rot and disintegrate.

2) Select materials that are only in perfect condition. Reject any faded or overblown flowers and wilting foliage. Imperfections in dried material always show up to a far greater degree than in fresh flowers and plants.

3) It is best to gather flowers before they reach full maturity. Fully-grown flowers tend to fade rapidly and can crumble very quickly.

Preserving plant material is not a hobby that needs to be restricted to the summer months. If weather conditions are favourable, many different flowers and foliage can be gathered all year round. After a while, a casual walk in the garden or countryside becomes an entirely different experience, searching for various plants and flowers to preserve.

AIR DRYING

Air drying (Fig. 63) is the simplest method of all used for preserving. It requires very little time and no sophisticated equipment. Many people only associate air drying with dried flowers. It is, however, a good choice for beginners or for those who do not have time to try the more specialised methods of preservation. Air drying is the most widely used method and many interesting and varied arrangements can be made using entirely air-dried materials. There are a number of variations for air drying although the principle remains the same. Air drying is the removal of moisture from the chosen plant or flower by the circulation of air.

Fig. 63 Air drying.

All that is required is a fairly large and airy space that has enough room to accommodate some hooks and a piece of string to hang the chosen material from. It should be cool, dry and dark. Lofts, sheds and garages are often suitable, although some tend to be damp. Bright light and warmth should be avoided as these conditions can produce faded and brittle results. Damp, clammy atmospheres are equally unsuitable as they can induce mildew. The most important factor that needs to be remembered with air drying is allowing enough space for the free circulation of air round *each* individual flower or plant. Large flowers are best dried individually, whereas small flowers can be arranged in tiny bunches. If space is a problem, a useful idea is to hang the flowers from wire coat hangers. These are the type supplied by dry cleaners and can be found breeding in most wardrobes!

After picking the material to be dried, remove the leaves from the stem and tie the stems together near the bottom. As the plant begins to lose moisture, the stems will start to shrink slightly. Instead of tying the bunches with string, it is far simpler to use either pipe cleaners or the metal ties used for sealing freezer bags. As the stems begin to shrink, the wire tie can be twisted and re-tightened. Elastic bands can also be useful for tying bunches of flowers together. String is used for tying and suspending the bunches from hooks or coat hangers in the drying area.

More coloured glass samples.

When drying flowers that either have no stems of their own, such as hollyhocks, or have very short stems, such as strawflowers, a substitute stem should be made before drying. Cut the stem down until it is about 2.5 cm (1 in) from the flowerhead. Insert a piece of florist's wire up through the stem and into the back of the flower. Care should be taken not to push the wire through the flowerhead. The wire can be placed in a block of oasis or a pot of sand to allow the plant to dry. As it does, it will shrink around the wire, holding it firmly in place.

127

A novel idea for air drying grasses is to place them in a suitable container, a vase or a jar, without any water. This encourages the natural curves to develop in the stems. Place them in similar conditions as before. Curved grasses are useful for the sides of arrangements. This is also an effective method when hanging space is unobtainable or in short supply. Although normally restricted to grasses, it can be used with flowers that have sufficiently strong stems, and the beauty of dried flowers is that it can cost nothing to experiment.

Another method is to hang small bunches of flowers, heads down, in an airing cupboard or a warm basement or attic, in fact anywhere that is warm, airy and dark with a good circulation of air. If an airing cupboard is used, it is best if the door is left slightly ajar to allow the air to circulate, otherwise the hot conditions can produce brittle flowers. Flowers that have rich, natural colours are best preserved by this method; these include Golden Rod (*Solidago*) and Love Lies Bleeding (*Amaranthus caudatus*). Using warmth the moisture is extracted more quickly and the beautiful colours of the flowers are preserved to a greater extent than using cool conditions. It is not advisable to preserve grasses by this method, however, as they tend to become very powdery and distintegrate.

DESICCANT POWDER DRYING

A large number of flowers can be preserved using this method (Fig. 64), although it is not usually employed for drying leaves, ferns and other foliage. It is a very useful means if space is a problem. All that is required is a number of cardboard boxes or tins large enough to accommodate the blooms, a drying agent, a small wire sieve or tea strainer and a warm place with enough space to store the containers. Flowers preserved by this method keep much of their original colour and shape far better than with conventional air-dried flowers. The only problem is that they are very delicate, almost tissue-paper-like. To overcome this it is often a good idea to reinforce the stems with florist's wire. This should be carried out before preserving the flower as its friable nature after treatment will make this extremely difficult.

The principle of this method is to use a desiccant drying powder which surrounds the flowers and rapidly dehydrates them, the moisture in the flowers being transferred to the powder. This is further accelerated by placing the container in a warm atmosphere. A number of powders are available. Ordinary domestic borax is still the most widely used, although silica gel, which is a relatively new material, is becoming popular due to its ability to absorb up to 50 per cent of its weight in water. Heat is unnecessary because of its moisture-absorbing properties. Silica gel is normally available in either powder or granular form. Powder is the best to use as silica gel is heavier than borax and in granular form its weight can distort the perfect shape of the more delicate flowers. Also, granules are difficult to sieve.

Silica gel, being such a good desiccant, tends to dry the hands and therefore it is always advisable to wear rubber gloves when handling it.

Fig. 64 Dessicant drying powder method.

After use, silica gel should be put in a shallow tray and placed in a warm oven at about 150°C (302°F) to dry out. Stir the powder occasionally to ensure even heat penetration. This process can take between two and four hours. While it is still warm, sift the powder into an airtight container and allow it to cool before re-using it. One other point worth mentioning is to seal the box or tin used for preserving with a lid and some sticky tape when using silica gel; otherwise it will continue to absorb the moisture in the atmosphere. As heat is not needed, the container can be stored in any suitable place during the preservation process.

Other drying agents that are often used are alum and even sand. If using sand, it is best to obtain silver sand as it is very fine and can be gently sifted onto the petals without crushing them. The sand must be completely dry. If there is any doubt it should be put in a shallow tray in a low oven temperature at about 130°C (266°F) for a couple of hours. Stir it from time to time to ensure that the sand is thoroughly dried. Being a heavy medium, sand is best used for the more robust flowerheads.

If difficulty is experienced in obtaining the above desiccants, salt or powdered starch can be used. Starch should be used with care as it sometimes clings to the petals. If this should happen, carefully brush away any that remains with a small sable-haired artist's brush. This applies when using any of the powders. Desiccant powder drying is not as straightforward as air drying, although the same rules apply when selecting subjects for preservation; namely that they must be completely free from moisture, especially rain or heavy dew. Use only flowers that are in perfect condition, as any imperfections will show in the end results. For beginners it is best to carry out a few experiments before hoping to achieve perfect results.

This form of preservation is very much a question of trial and error, but once a good result is obtained it will be shown to be well worthwhile. During the experimental period it is best to use an inexpensive drying agent such as borax, as silica gel tends to be more expensive.

Daffodils and daisy-like flowers are often favoured by the beginner. Prepare the flowers as with air drying. They must be freshly picked; it is of no use preserving flowers that have been placed in a vase for several days and then deciding to dry them, as they are bound to be past their best by then. If buying from a florist, ensure that the blossoms are in first class condition and not beginning to droop and fade. Strip all of the foliage from the flower. Make sure that the stems are dry and moisture-free. Choose a shallow box or tin of a suitable size, large enough to accommodate the flowers without overcrowding them. To prevent the powder spilling over the work surface it is best to stand the box inside a larger one to catch any surplus powder. Spoon a layer of powder onto the box to a depth of about 13 mm (½ in) and carefully arrange the flowers in the box. They should be close together but it is better if they do not overlap. It is a good policy not to mix the varieties of flowers to be dried if at all possible, as some can take a longer period to dry than others.

Using the wire sieve, gently sift more powder over the flowers ensuring that each individual petal has a good covering of powder. For smaller flowers a tea strainer may be found to be easier for the sifting. Continue in this way until all of the flowers are completely covered. Take the box and place it in a warm place such as a heated basement or an airing cupboard. The amount of time that the powder takes to remove the moisture from the petals will greatly depend on the size of the flower. Small flowers with uncomplicated shapes, such as daisies and pansies, may take only a couple of days. Tiny flowers may be dried in as little as 24 hours. More complex subjects such as roses may require at least a week or more to dry out completely.

After a few days check to see if the flowers are dry. Taking great care, gently brush away a little powder from the petals and see if any moisture is present. If it is, re-cover and wait another couple of days and re-test until there is no moisture present. Leave the blossoms in the powder for another day or so to be absolutely sure. A great deal of care should be taken when removing the flowers from the drying powder, due to their delicate state. Spoon away some of the powder covering the stem, then insert the spoon under each flower in turn and lift them out. Gently tap the stems to remove any surplus powder. If any does adhere to the petals, brush it off using a sable artist's brush. Due to their fragile nature, desiccant dried flowers need to be stored with a lot of care, either by arranging them in a block of oasis placed on the shelf of a cupboard in dry, dark conditions, or carefully placed in a stout cardboard box with a few granules of either borax or silica gel to absorb any moisture in the atmosphere.

GLYCERINE PRESERVATION

Glycerine preservation (Fig. 65) is used for preserving various pieces of foliage including ferns and grasses. Flowers and seed heads are not normally preserved by this method, although there are a few exceptions.

The basic principle involved is that the water in the plant is replaced by the glycerine solution which is drawn up the stem by capillary action. This method can produce some very interesting and attractive results. As the glycerine is absorbed many specimens tend to change colour slightly. Green beech leaves acquire a darker olive green colour and, if exposed to light, will begin to turn a light shade of tan. Glycerine-preserved foliage remains far more supple and pliable than material that has been preserved in the more conventional manner. Its other advantage is its ability to retain its original three-dimensional form. As with any method of preservation, it is best to choose material in first-class condition. Deciduous (the name given to trees and shrubs that shed their leaves annually) foliage should be gathered before it begins to change colour in late autumn. Evergreen foliage can be preserved at any time of the year. If leaves are in large bunches, strip some of them off to leave a more uncluttered arrangement. Split or crush the bottom of the stems; about 5 cm (2 in) should be sufficient. This will help the plant to absorb the glycerine solution.

Make a solution of one part glycerine to two parts boiling water. It is important to use hot water as glycerine mixes easier with this than with cold. Mix the solution together thoroughly, using a wooden spoon or a piece of wood. Glycerine is heavier than water, and if it is not completely dissolved there is a tendency for the plant to absorb water instead of the glycerine mixture. Allow the mixture to cool. Pour the solution into a narrow, deep container. This should be capable of holding the stems of the material to be preserved. Cover them to a depth of 7.5 cm (3 in).

Place the plants and the container into a larger container of sufficient size to support the foliage and prevent it falling over. The time needed for the plant or foliage to absorb enough of the glycerine to preserve it depends mostly on individual specimens, their leaf size and the time during their growing cycle that they were gathered. A branch with very small leaves can absorb the mixture within a couple of days, whereas longer-leafed varieties can take a lot longer (four to five weeks in some

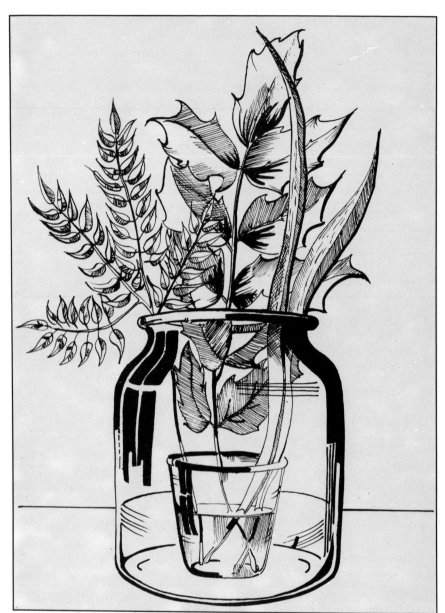

Fig. 65 Glycerine preservation method.

cases). Inspect the leaves regularly; the glycerine solution can often be observed being absorbed into the veins on the back of the leaves.

Remember to top up the solution at regular intervals. When the leaves begin to sweat, rub them between the fingers and, if they have a sheen to them and feel oily, the glycerine solution has been absorbed. Take them from the solution and wipe any moisture from them. Store them in a box placed in a cool, dark place. Do not store too much material in any one box as this will flatten the foliage.

PRESERVING BY PRESSING

Ferns, leaves and small flowers intended for use in pictures or sandwiched between two sheets of glass for trinket boxes are easily pressed and dried between two sheets of blotting paper (Fig. 66). Select the items to be pressed, ensuring that they are freshly picked and free from any moisture. Carefully arrange them on a sheet of blotting paper, or if none is available use newspaper. Making sure that they do not overlap place the other sheet over them, checking to ensure that nothing has moved. Slide the sheets between several layers of newspaper, and slide the newspaper under a piece of carpet that is frequently walked upon. Ensure that the wad of newspaper is thick enough to give sufficient protection to prevent the pattern of the carpet backing being embossed onto the pressed material.

In these affluent times of fitted carpets, many homes do not have loose carpets. An alternative method, therefore, is to sandwich the blotting paper in the middle of an old telephone directory or large book and place a

Fig. 66 Preserving by pressing.

suitable heavy weight on top; a couple of bricks would be quite suitable. Keep in a dry place for roughly two to three weeks until the leaves feel completely dry to the touch.

For instant results it is well worth experimenting by taking some leaves of ferns, placing them between a couple of sheets of newspaper and running a warm iron over them. The iron is best used on a very cool setting. These instant dried leaves and ferns will not last as long as the more conventionally dried pieces, no longer than four to six weeks normally, but they can make an ideal display if time is important.

FLOWERS TO PRESERVE

Half-hardy annuals (HHA) need to be germinated either in a greenhouse or on a windowsill in early spring. For early flowering a warm greenhouse is needed and the seeds are sown from mid-winter to mid-spring. Many half-hardy annuals can be successfully grown in open ground from late spring onwards.

Hardy annuals (HA) can be grown in open ground from early spring until early summer, the earlier the better, though, providing that the soil is warm. Thin them out as they mature to avoid overcrowding.

Hardy perennials (HP) come into flower about a year after they are sown. Seed should be sown in spring and early summer in open ground. Germination is sometimes slow and erratic. Certain varieties can take as long as six months to start growing until the seeds have been subjected to frost. They generally grow better in a prepared seed bed that has been raked to a fine tilth.

Also included in the following list are some *hardy biennials* (HB), which flower in the second year and *hardy shrubs* (HS).

Acanthus (Bear's Breeches) (HA). White and rose purple. Preserve by air drying.

Achillea (HP). Yellow, cerise, pink and white. Preserve by air drying.

Acrolinium (HA). Pink, rose, red, white. Preserve by air drying.

Althaea (Hollyhock) (HP). Crimson, rose pink, scarlet, yellow and white. Preserve with desiccant drying powder. Lay on its side.

Amaranthus (Love Lies Bleeding) (HA). Crimson, green. Preserve by air drying.

Anemone (HP). Blue, mauve, pink, scarlet. Preserve by using desiccant drying powder. Lay on its side.

Calendula (HA). Various shades of yellow and orange. Preserve using desiccant drying powder. Lay face down.

Camellia (HS). Pink, red and white. Preserve using desiccant drying powder. Lay face up.

Centauria (Cornflowers) (HA). Blue, pink, maroon and red. Preserve using desiccant drying powder. Lay face down. Strengthen stem before preserving.

Dahlia (HHA or tuber). Yellow, pink, rose, scarlet and white. Preserve using desiccant drying powder. Lay face down.

Delphinium (HP). Purple, blue, yellow and pink. Preserve either by air drying or using desiccant drying power. Also in this genus is Larkspur (HA) – pink, mauve, cerise, white. Preserve by air drying.

Gentiana (HP). Blue. Preserve using desiccant drying powder. Lay on its side.

Gypsophila (Baby's Breath) (HP). White. Preserve by air drying.

Helichrysum (Strawflower) (HHA). Scarlet, crimson, yellow. Preserve by air drying.

Hydrangea (HS). Blue, pink. Preserve by standing it in water and then allowing to dry out.

Moluccella (Bells of Ireland) (HA). White. Preserve using desiccant drying powder, air drying or glycerine.

Myosotis (Forget-me-not) (HB). Blue, pink. Preserve using desiccant drying powder. Lay face up.

Narcissus (including Daffodils) (Bulbs). Yellow and white. Preserve using desiccant drying powder. Lay face up. Strengthen stem before preserving.

Nigella (Love-in-the-Mist) (HA). Blue, rose pink. Preserve using desiccant drying powder. Lay face down.

Phlox drummondii (HHA), Blue, violet, crimson, scarlet, pink. Preserve by air drying.

Physalis (Chinese Lanterns) (HP). Orange, red. Preserve by air drying.

Rosa (HS). Various colours. Preserve by either air drying or using desiccant drying powder. Lay face down.

Saxifraga (HP). White, pink, rose. Preserve by using desiccant drying powder. Lay face down.

Sedum (HP). Yellow, pink, red. Preserve by air drying.

Solidago (Golden Rod) (HP). Yellow. Preserve by air drying.

Statice (HP). White, lavender, mauve. Preserve by air drying.

Tagetes (Marigolds) (HHA). Yellow. Preserve using desiccant drying powder. Lay face down.

Viola (including Pansies) (HHA). White, mauve, yellow. Preserve using desiccant drying powder. Lay face up.

Zinnia (HHA). Gold, cream, rose, orange, scarlet, carmine, pink. Preserve by air drying or using desiccant drying powder. Lay face down.

8 Turning a Pastime into a Profit

There are a number of ways to sell the finished product. Obviously, the best place to start is on your own doorstep, selling to friends, relatives and neighbours. The best and cheapest form of advertising is by recommendation.

It is an advantage at an early stage to try and have a leaflet or brochure printed, illustrating the different designs available. Printing need not be expensive and it helps to show terrariums and planters to a wider public. Many people do not really know what a terrarium is and many think it is a place for keeping terrapins! With a leaflet these misconceptions can be dispelled. Another good idea is to have some plant care labels printed which mention the maker's name. As more and more copperfoil projects are completed, each one of a higher standard than the last, friends, family and colleagues will begin to show an interest and it will begin to be realised that, unlike many other hobbies, terrarium manufacture can be turned into a profitable pastime. Not only can this help to pay for more materials and tools but it is also an advantage to keep selling items as they are made so that other ideas and designs may be attempted. The scope for innovation in terrarium design is endless. Some of these have been touched on in other chapters. Etched, engraved and stained glass make attractive gifts on their own but, when incorporated in a terrarium with an attractive background of houseplants or dried flowers, the result can be stunning. A small pump of the type used in fishponds can provide a miniature waterfall. The limit to possible ideas is only your imagination.

One factor that it is worth remembering at all times when pricing work for re-sale is that terrariums and copperfoil projects in general are very labour-intensive; sometimes ten to fifteen hours may be spent on one item. It is far better to price the finished product at a higher price than a lower one. It is easy to bring the price down if need be, but not so simple to raise it. Selling cheaply will not reflect the time and care that has been taken in the making. Also, there is the danger that demand will outstrip supplies.

TEACHING

It comes as a surprise to many that ordinary, unqualified people can teach at adult education centres in some subjects. This is in fact true. Many centres are looking for new and diverse courses to be included in future prospectuses and to encourage new students. Once the craft has been mastered to a high enough standard teaching it can be contemplated. The Principal of the local adult education centre should be approached. It is a wise precaution to make enquiries to ensure that there is not already a course in progress.

Many colleges and centres run short courses for new teachers to help them learn to teach more effectively, once a course has been running successfully.

PARTY SELLING

Party selling is a popular method of selling any number of products from plastic food containers to exotic lingerie. It is a popular form of retailing, as apart from supplying some food and drink there is very little outlay. It is best to arrange a party in your own home at first and then try to persuade friends and neighbours to hold one, offering either a commission on items sold or a free gift such as a smaller terrarium.

The items to be sold should be reasonably inexpensive, such as small terrariums and planters and perhaps a few trinket boxes. Display larger items but do not expect to sell them. Many people go to this kind of party more out of politeness than with the intention of purchasing expensive goods, although some will remember them and very often purchase at a later date for a special gift.

CRAFT FAIRS

Craft fairs can be a useful venue for displaying terrariums and copperfoil products, although the success of many of them will depend to a large extent on the organisers and the amount of advertising and promotion that the event has had.

As with party selling, it is best to take along some fairly inexpensive items. The general public do not normally attend craft fairs with the intention of spending a lot of money, although of course there are exceptions. One of the bonuses of craft fairs is the opportunity to meet and talk with fellow stallholders who are very often interesting craftsmen in their own right. Forthcoming events are often advertised in local papers or magazines.

RETAIL SHOPS

Retail shops such as garden centres, florists and craft shops would seem to be an ideal outlet for selling terrariums and other plant-related items. This is generally true, but one factor should be borne in mind before approaching them. Retail shops have very high overheads and require a reasonable profit on any items that they sell. This 'profit margin' can vary between 30 per cent and 100 per cent. Garden centres frequently put on a higher profit margin for plants and flowers as they are perishable and can lose their sales appeal if they begin to fade. This is equally true of terrariums. Also, being a new item, the sales potential is unknown. A way around this is to offer the products on a sale-or-return basis in return for a lower profit margin. It can be inconvenient to have stock tied up in this way, but as the sales potential is seen a normal trading relationship can be set up.

ADVERTISING

Advertising can be a very hit and miss affair. Someone once said of advertising that only 50 per cent of it is effective and he wished that he could find out which half it was. This is very true.

If the budget runs to it, it is best if a semi-display advert is used, as a small picture of a terrarium can be shown and this will have more impact than a lineage advert. As advertising is expensive, it is best to plan a campaign around peak present-buying times such as Christmas.

A useful form of free advertising is to use a device called a press release. This is usually a short article extolling the virtues of the product which is sent to any relevant publications in the hope that they will take an interest and publish it.

One final point that is worth bearing in mind, whichever approach is used for marketing and selling the finished product, is that it is best to try to show a professional businesslike approach, even if the workshop consists of a kitchen table. Money spent on printing letterheads, leaflets, business cards etc is well worthwhile. Also it is an advantage at an early stage to keep a set of books. This is not as daunting as it sounds, as all that is needed is a set of exercise books: one for the purchase ledger, which are the items bought for manufacture, stationery etc; another for the sales ledger, which is simply a record of items sold, and so on. A set of simple books is a must if you really want to turn a pastime into profit, and run it as a small business.

Appendix: Suppliers

UNITED KINGDOM

Copperfoil Enterprises, 141 Lyndhurst Drive, Hornchurch, Essex RM11 1JP, Tel: 04024 56697

Glass Houses, 59 Station Road, Tempsford, Bedfordshire SG19 2AU. Tel: 0767 40235

James Hetley & Company Limited, 11 Beresford Avenue, Wembley, Middlesex. Tel: 01 903 4151

Lead and Light, Commercial Place, Camden Lock, London NW1 8AF. Tel: 01 485 4568

Stained Glass Supplies, Unit 5, Brunel Way, Thornbury Industrial Estate, Bristol BS12 2UR. Tel: 0454 419975

Swiss Glass Engraving Limited, Maylite Trading Estate, Martley, Worcestershire WR6 6PQ. Tel: 08866 226

The Glass Market, The Old Mill House, Temple, Marlow, Bucks SL7 1SA. Tel: 062 882 4900

AUSTRALIA

Lillydale Leadlight Studio, Cnr. Hutchinson & John Streets, Lilydale, Victoria 3140. Tel: 7354156

Moorabbin Glass (Holdings) Pty. Limited, 234 Centre Dandenong Road, Cheltenham, Victoria 3192. Tel: 5846733

Southern Craft House, 477 Glenhuntly Road, Elsternwick 3185, Victoria. Tel: 528 4832

Yencken Sandy Glass Industries, 98–102 Gaffney Street, Coburg, Victoria 3058. Tel: 3543631

UNITED STATES OF AMERICA

Big M Stained Glass, 5903 Corson Avenue South, Seattle, Washington 98108. Tel: (800) 426 8307

Ed Hoys Stained Glass, 999 E. Chicago Avenue, Naperville, Illinois 60504. Tel: (800) 323 5668

Houston Stained Glass, 5151 Broadway, Oakland CA. 94611. Tel: (800) 231 0148

Hudson Glass Company Inc, 219C N. Division Street, Peekskill, N.Y. 10566. Tel: (800) 431 2964

Whittemore-Durgin Glass Company, Post Office Box 2065, Hanover, Massachusetts 02339. Tel: (617) 871–1743

Bibliography

Arnold, Jud, *The Illustrated Encyclopedia of House Plants* Ward Lock Limited 1979.

Ashberry, Anne, *Bottle Gardens & Fern Cases* Hodder & Stoughton 1964.

Bonar, Ann *The Complete Guide to Indoor Gardening* Octopus Books Ltd 1983.

Burgoyne, Ian, & Scoble, Rachel, *Two Thousand Years of Flat Glass Making* Pilkington Brothers 1983.

Huxley, Anthony, *House Plants, Cacti and Succulents* Hamlyn 1972.

McHoy, Peter, *House Plants: A Complete Guide to Indoor Gardening* Octopus Books Ltd 1981.

Odell, Olive, *Country Crafts Dried Flowers* Hamlyn 1979.

Wickers, David, *Indoor Farming* Julian Friedmann Publishers Limited 1977.

Foster, Maureen, *Flower Preserving for Beginners* Pelham Books 1977.

Glossary

ABRADING Wearing away by friction.

ALLOY A mixture of two or more metals.

ANNEALING Controlled cooling of glass to relieve stresses.

ANNUAL A plant that grows from seed, flowers and completes its life cycle in one year.

BREAKING OUT Removing surplus glass from the piece being shaped by tapping, grozing etc.

BURNISHING Rubbing and smoothing down.

CRIMPING Folding and pressing the copperfoil tape onto the glass.

CUTTING A portion of stem, leaf or root removed from a plant, treated and planted to propagate new plants.

DESICCANT A material that absorbs water and is used to remove moisture when drying flowers etc.

FILIGREE Delicate, ornate shapes often made from brass or copper wire.

FIRE-POLISHED Glass that has a natural brilliant finish without the need of mechanical polishing.

FLUX A substance that removes the oxide that can form on copperfoil and helps the fusion between the metal and the solder.

A FORMER A mould used to help shape the glass cylinder.

A GATHER Molten glass that is collected from the furnace and placed on the end of the blowpipe before being blown.

GERMINATION The initiation of growth in a seed.

HALF-HARDY This describes plants that need special protection from frost and low temperatures.

HARDY This describes plants that can survive in the open throughout the year and are not affected by frost.

HEAT SINK A piece of metal used to absorb and radiate heat away from the soldering iron tip.

HORTAG A commercial man-made pebble-shaped aggregate.

LEHR A long, tunnel-shaped oven used for the controlled cooling of glass.

MOUTHBLOWN The original method of flat glass manufacture.

OASIS A sponge-like substance used as a base for flower arranging. Easily cut it can be used wet or dry.

OXIDISATION The action of air on metal, resulting in the formation of a film of oxide.

PATINA A thin film that forms on the surface of the solder and changes its colour.

PERENNIAL A plant that lives for two years or more, usually for an indefinite period, and flowers every year.

PROPAGATION The reproduction of plants by taking cuttings etc.

RESIST A material painted on glass when etching to prevent chemical reaction taking place where it is not required.

RHIZOME A fleshy underground stem which normally lasts for more than one year.

RUN A controlled crack in a piece of glass.

TINNING Coating with solder.

TUSCHE A thin acid-resistant paint.

WASTING Uneven thickness in glass.

Index

Figures in **bold** refer to colour illustrations, and those in italics to black and white.